PENTECOST
and the Chosen One

Also by W J Corbett

The Bear who Stood on his Head
Dear Grumble
Duck Soup Farm
The End of the Tale
The Grandson Boy
Little Elephant
Toby's Iceberg

for older readers

The Song of Pentecost
(Winner of the Whitbread Award)
Pentecost of Lickey Top

W.J. CORBETT

PENTECOST
and the Chosen One

Illustrated by Martin Ursell

MAMMOTH

First published in Great Britain 1984
by Methuen Children's Books Ltd
Published 1995 by Mammoth
an imprint of Reed Consumer Books Ltd
Michelin House, 81, Fulham Road, London SW3 6RB
and Auckland, Melbourne, Singapore and Toronto

Text copyright © 1984 W.J. Corbett
Illustrations copyright © 1984 Martin Ursell

ISBN 0 7497 1850 1

A CIP catalogue record for this title
is available from the British Library

Printed in Great Britain by
BPC Paperbacks Ltd
A member of
The British Printing Company Ltd

Contents

Contents

1 *The Shadow of a Hero*

'One day the world will learn the truth,' yelled Owl of Lickey Top, wincing as pain shot through his bad toe. 'And when it does all hedgehogs will be forever branded as two-faced scoundrels, and destroyers of the country-side.'

The old hedgehog took not the slightest notice. He continued to utter small grunts of pleasure as he rooted for snails at the foot of the bird's tree. It was the young hedgehog, his son, who replied. 'You can hope all you wish,' he said, his tone cool as he stared up into Owl's angry face. 'But be warned, this bit of the world is becoming sick and tired of your constant complaining. As for the rest of it, folk will soon learn that owls tend to make much ado about nothing. For the fair-minded will surely agree that my dad, the Old Codger, is per-fectly entitled to enjoy a last supper in the land of his birth. Or a last lunch, should he decide to die around mid-day.'

'Over my dead body,' Owl screeched. 'I don't care where you were born.' Tears squeezed from his sleepless eyes. 'Everyone knows the suffering I endured as a chick,' he wept. 'The world shared my pain when I was banished from home, and forced to carve out a new life as a lonely recluse, here on Lickey Top. Yet despite all that, didn't I offer the Pentecost mouse and his family a home when they had nowhere else to go? Yet this is my reward. To be laid low with a seriously in-growing toe-nail, unable to defend my property against a pair of scheming hedgehogs who are rapidly churning it into a quagmire.'

'My dad, the Old Codger, cannot be held responsible for the fickleness of fate,' came the sharp reply. 'Why, he isn't even responsible for himself . . . I am.'

'The world will judge your actions,' bellowed Owl. 'It will also call to account the Pentecost mouse who, instead of sorting out this crisis, seems more interested in gazing at himself in puddles. Make no mistake, the time is fast approaching for those who would do me down.'

'Talking about time,' said the young hedgehog, cocking an eye at the sun, 'I hope you've quite finished, for dang me if it won't be tea-time in two ticks.' So saying, he nudged his father towards a likely-looking nettle-bed. Only when he was satisfied that the Old Codger was taking nourishment did he bury his own blunt nose into the lush roots. Owl groaned his pain and frustration, slumped back into the dark confines of his home, and drifted off into an uneasy slumber.

'Poor old Owl,' whispered a softly gleeful voice. The Cockle Snorkle, glowing happily, came stealing in to view his master. He continued in a mock-solemn voice, 'Oh wicked fate to drag my twitching friend so low. But I'll stand by him. And if the disbelieving world should jeer my words, I'll grin and sneer, for soon I go to cheer the brooding Pentecost mouse. . . .'

High upon a hill a small Harvest mouse sat watching the clouds drift by and dreaming of secret longings. Pentecost was no ordinary mouse. His brain was clever and quick, and it was for this reason he had been chosen as the new leader of the family. But these days Pentecost didn't care much about leadership. He paid little heed to the arguments raging on Lickey Top. In truth he felt too dispirited to care. The danger signs, the mounting tension on Lickey Top, he chose to ignore. These days he seemed to have retreated into a private world of his own.

Autumn had come to the Lickey Hills. A whole season had passed since the tragic death of the old Pentecost. He it was, who, with a little help from his friend Fox of Furrowfield, had led the harvest mouse family from the over-spilling city to this new home in the Lickey Hills. Now that brave mouse lay at rest beneath the earth, his memory forever alive in the hearts of his loved ones.

For a time after the old Pentecost's death the new leader, happy and proud to be chosen, had set about his responsible tasks with a will. He had organised the building of the new homes, flattered their landlord Owl to keep him sweet, and was pleased to settle the odd squabble that Uncle, an annoying old mouse, seemed to delight in starting. But soon things started to go wrong for the eager new Pentecost. With all the work completed, the urgency and the excitement of the fresh start ebbed away. The harvest mice, secure and contented now, seemed not to need his advice and guidance quite so often. The small mice, as youngsters everywhere, wished only to roll down the gentle slopes of Lickey Top, and explore dangerous places. The older mice enjoyed relaxing now, the aunts ever talking nostalgically of days gone by as they busily spun their grass-stems into interesting shapes. The subject of conversation was always the same: how the old Pentecost had led them to this promised land, only to die at journey's end.

The new Pentecost would steal miserably away to brood alone upon his hill, feeling unneeded and useless. And time and again his downcast eyes would turn to view that carefully tended mound a short way down the hill, the grave of that hero in whose shadow he lived.

It seemed no unhappiness was spared him. There was also the question of Fox. Ever since that night in the Weasel Woods, shortly after Pentecost had been hailed as the new leader, and where Fox had spoken so kindly to him, the mouse had believed he had made a close friend for life. His hope had been that one day he would come to replace the old Pentecost in Fox's affections. But his dream seemed not to be. Though Fox sometimes popped up to Lickey Top, Pentecost came to believe he detected a coolness and reserve in Fox's tone when they spoke together. Being a sensitive soul, Pentecost took this to be a sign of disfavour. Soon bitterness crept into his heart as he became more and more convinced that Fox, and indeed everyone, was against him. And he was certain he knew why. Fox and the family could only be secretly comparing him with the old Pentecost, and doubtless whispering that he himself was a boring mouse, fit only to be humoured and pitied. But what could he do about it? How could he ever prove himself the equal of the old leader in these times of peace and plenty? How could he make Fox and the family see that he was really a get-up-and-go mouse, without an adventure to test his mettle? These were the reasons why Pentecost sat alone upon the hill, wishing the world was a fairer place, and feeling much too sorry for himself.

This isolation only served to increase his discontent. Soon he took to gazing into puddles at his looks. He did not like what he saw. He hated his long and comically drooping ears. What chance had he to become a respected hero with such a handicap, he grieved? Then his bitterness would spill over. It was all the fault of Uncle, he thought savagely. He remembered that time when the old mouse had meddled with them just outside Woodpecker Wood, on the journey to the new home on Lickey Top. His ears had become hopelessly blocked with saw-dust and Uncle had attempted to 'cure' them. Instead he had succeeded in ruining their shape for life. The fact that the old Pentecost had possessed oddly coloured eyes, and yet had risen above them, never occurred to him. Filled with self-pity, Pentecost saw in that puddle an unwanted and tedious mouse, with more than his share of unattractive features. In short a washed-up leader, without a mission in life. Not even the arrival of strangers on Lickey Top could rouse him from his sullen mood. Not even when they began to sow discord, create havoc, and lead Uncle and the young mice astray. Had he been a responsible mouse he would have recognised all the danger signs and acted. But he wasn't, so he didn't. . . .

The Old Codger and Son had just returned from a complete trip around the world. Or so they said. They also declared that as Lickey Top had been the old hedgehog's starting point, the trip should properly end there. Or rather the Son declared it, for his father's mouth was constantly engaged with chewing lunch, and other meals. According to the Son the Old Codger had been born on Owl's property, and now, feeling the aches and pains of advanced age, had decided to end his days there. Reasonable enough, but there were problems. It appeared Owl and the Old Codger were mortal enemies from way back. No matter that their paths had not crossed in many a long day. Even when separated by perhaps half a world, their hatred each for the other had continued to burn fiercely bright. One reason for this enmity was fleas. Unfortunately the old hedgehog simply jumped with them, and Owl, a fussily clean bird had a horror of creepy-crawlies. At the mere mention of fleas he would claw himself raw. So when father and son were spied loitering about the edge of the Weasel Woods, Owl firmly put his foot down. The Old Codger and Son were warned to venture no further than the tree-line under pain of death. But fleas apart, there were other reasons that kept Owl's hatred thriving. One was the Old Codger's enormous appetite for snails. There was nothing he loved more than to rout and browse amongst nettle-beds, in search of those delicious whirly-shelled creatures. Unfortunately, he had a complete disregard for tidiness. In a very short time he was able to reduce the prettiest of spots into a moonscape. And, no fool, he knew the nettle-beds of Lickey Top abounded with his favourite dish.

'I'm not having my property churned about like a tip,' yelled Owl from his hole in the rock. 'Hop it, and take your fleas with you.'

'My dad is entitled to die on a full stomach,' shouted back the enraged Son, from the edge of the woods. 'How dare you make his mouth water by allowing good food to go to waste?'

But Owl was not to be moved. In fact, he was so determined to keep his enemy at bay, he took to staying up days. Even though red-eyed through lack of rest, he never ceased his vigil. For their part, the harvest mice thought he was going a little over the top. But as yet, they didn't know what the bird knew. For he had a much more important reason for keeping that prickly pair off Lickey Top. A deeply superstitious soul, he was

6

well aware that the Old Codger was no ordinary hedgehog. . . .

The Old Codger had been born with 'the gift'. Once when very young, he had remarked quite casually that 'someone was soon to tumble down a steep drop, and hit his head upon a rock'. The prophecy had scarcely left his mouth before an ancient relative suddenly vanished into a gully, to reappear with a large bump on his crown. From that day forth the Old Codger was avoided like the plague. Understandable, for who wished to know the worst before it happened? Who wished to suffer the double agony of knowing one was about to be injured, plus the experience itself? Not surprising then, that he became an outcast, cursed to wander the world, forever despised. Luckily he fathered a son on his travels. This small kindness of fate proved a boon amidst a scorning universe. Without his son's staunchly loyal company, the Old Codger would have long ago gone mad. For he had acquired not only a son, but a mouthpiece too. The Son was fiercely proud of his gifted father.

'Is it too much to ask?' the Son, hiding behind the bole of a tree, shouted indignantly. 'A plague upon your gloomy abode, you miserly Owl!'

His anger continued to fall on deaf ears. Owl, eyes aching with fatigue, nevertheless remained alert. So long as he lived, the Old Codger would not set a muddy paw on his beloved land. The cockle-snorkle, his constant companion, was of a like mind. As Owl's eyes dipped in sleep from time to time, he was there at his ear, urging the bird to hold out. It was a battle of wills. At the moment Owl was winning. But not for long. In the meantime the harvest mice were viewing this argy-bargy with mixed feelings. Most of them felt rather sorry for the Old Codger and Son. But on the other hand, now happily settled into their new home, they feared to upset their landlord Owl. Once they broached the problem to their leader, Pentecost, but to no avail. Hugging his selfish worries close, he had all but turned his back upon the world.

Then came the day when Owl's worst fears were realised. The Son, prompted by his father, shouted from the edge of the Weasel Woods that something was about to turn up for Owl, which the very next day it did. Exactly at sunrise the bird went down with a badly in-growing toe-nail. Racked with pain, he barely managed to stock in a little extra food before collapsing on his back in the hole in the oak. Roundly cursing the Old Codger and his gift, he settled down to sweat it out. His faith was touching indeed. He would whisper between groans to the cockle-snorkle, 'That which curves inwards, is bound to curve outwards again, sooner or later'. For he was aware that the laws of the universe applied equally to owls. So, sprawled on his back in his dank home, and staring in saucer-eyed horror at his foot, he waited for fate to smile upon him once more.

This was the moment the hedgehogs had been waiting for. Eagerly they advanced up the hill, their eyes sparkling as they spied the nettle-beds of Lickey Top, abundantly crammed with the goodies that dreams are made of. Without more ado they tucked in. Thus began a lunch-time that would only end when the sun went down. Then, precisely at dusk commenced supper-time, that leisurely meal ending on the dot of sunrise. Typically, breakfast and tea-time were scorned, for hedgehogs never went in for tasty snacks between meals. They believed that only greedy folk indulged themselves so. It was during a rare pause to allow their

stomachs to settle when they spoke to their first harvest mouse. It happened to be old Uncle, easily the silliest member of his family. With his weakness for flattery, he was soon staunchly loyal to the pair. The Son's kind remarks about the silvery sweep of his whiskers made the old fool's head swim with pleasure. After he had listened to the young hedgehog's sad tale concerning their worldly wanderings, tears came swiftly to Uncle's eyes. He was hooked, and good.

'Is it not reasonable?' he argued to doubting family members. 'The Old Codger is on his way out, and wishes only to snuff it in the land of his birth. Who is so wicked as to deny this last request?'

Owl was that wicked, and managed to groan so, his bleary head lolling from his hollow home. But his weak protests were drowned by Uncle's strident argument. 'We all have to go sometime,' he warned. 'Time ticks away even for sickly owls.'

This last was aimed to unnerve the bird, which it did. Owl, his throbbing foot hanging over the edge of the hole, could only fret and fume, and threaten terrible revenge when he regained his health and strength. Helplessly, he glared down at the hated enemy, now chomping contentedly at the foot of his tree.

Throughout all the comings and goings and arguments, Pentecost still sat alone upon the hill. It was as if he had withdrawn into the most private of shells. Apart from the occasional glance into a puddle he spent most of his time sighing, and staring at the drifting clouds. It could be said, quite fairly, that he was well on the way to becoming a totally ruined mouse. For surely a leader of worth would have attempted to settle the quarrels that threatened to tear Lickey Top apart? But for Pentecost, the world outside seemed not to matter any more. It so happened the mouse was puddle-gazing when Fox arrived much out of breath. Quickly, Pentecost averted his eyes from the waters. Too late . . . .

A little earlier, down in Furrowfields, Fox had been feeling particularly tense. Though he had been careful to behave normally in the presence of his cubs, his mate, curled up and watching from the mouth of their lair knew what was going through his mind. For once again old yearnings had returned to plague him. He had become bored with the sameness of everyday life. The desire to pit his wits and skills against the world had surfaced yet again. Before the day was out Fox would answer that call.

Suddenly, without a word, he was up and off. He ran to take his mind off the coming night, his speed never slackening despite the thump of his heart, loud in his ears. Only when he had climbed the One Hundred Steps did he stop to rest. There on the smooth Plateau he sat gazing about, gulping down huge lungfuls of air, feeling never more alive. And always that sensation was there, not quite fear, but that certain thrilling chill he could not live without for long. Exhilarated, he threw back his head and howled, a challenge eagerly returned from the echoing hills. Then he was on his feet and off again, higher and higher, to see a friend with whom to while away the restless hours till nightfall. . . .

'And who is the fairest of us all?' Fox said. Then with a grin, 'Isn't all this reflecting rather a waste of time? Puddles never lie, small conceited mouse.'

'I was merely trying to judge the depth,' lied Pentecost. He continued sadly, 'You wouldn't have greeted the old Pentecost in such a hurtful manner.'

'Yes, I would,' answered Fox quickly. 'For he had a

sense of humour. So what's happened to yours? Don't think I haven't noticed all the grumpy sighing and sky-gazing these past few weeks. So what's the problem?'

'Do you really want to know?' said Pentecost, squaring his shoulders, and looking Fox in the eye. 'Very well, if I can hold your interest long enough. Deny that you feel I am not a patch on the old Pentecost. Admit that you think me the most boring of mice. Tell me to my face that you only come up here when you have nothing better to do . . . and please don't stare at my ears in that way.'

'Why?' replied Fox, with a twinkle. 'I think they are very attractive, but all right, if you insist that this is grievance-airing time. For a start, you are talking utter rubbish. Not a patch on the old Pentecost? So what do you want to be, a carbon-copy? Boring? You *are* in danger of becoming boring if you continue along these lines. And the reason why I come up here? Well, for a bit of peace and quiet, if you must know. And your company perfectly fits the bill. You are a nice, quiet, pottering mouse, and my fondness increases by leaps and bounds. . . .'

'In other words, I am without zip,' said a bitter Pentecost. 'You say you are fond of me yet you have just rained me with insults. How would you like to be called a 'pottering' fox? Don't you realise I am at heart an adventurous mouse, ready at a moment's notice to stride out at your side in search of danger?'

'Leaving Lickey Top to go to pot,' observed a wry Fox, glancing down the hill. He continued, 'I heard right, then? The Old Codger and Son have given up world travel? So what are you doing sitting here feeling sorry for yourself? Never mind about striding off in search of danger, for if my guess is correct, you'll have your work cut out keeping this place in order. Lickey Top is beginning to look like a rubbish tip already. And I hear Owl is out of action, too? So when are you going to stride down this hill, and do a bit of leading, as you were chosen to do?'

Pentecost was suddenly haughty. 'Don't poke your nose where it isn't wanted,' he warned. 'Everything is under control up here.'

'Yes, but under whose control?' said Fox. 'I'm telling you these things for your own good. For Heaven's sake, pull yourself together and snap out of this dream-world of yours. You yearn to be a mouse with zip? Then zip amongst that lot down there before it's too late.'

'The family don't need me,' replied Pentecost, his tone filled with self-pity. 'They only wish to sit about discussing the bravery of another mouse. And you – you just wish to get me off your back with your scare-mongering. You just don't want me tagging along on the adventure you are planning. But your subtle wiles don't fool me, Fox.'

Fox became annoyed. 'Do you know what subtle means?' he snapped. 'I ask because I'm beginning to think you are not the Pentecost mouse for the job.'

'It means a mouse of craft and acute awareness,' said Pentecost, quickly. 'In fact, the perfect companion for an adventure-seeking fox. . . .'

'Crafty and sly,' corrected the other. 'And I should know, for I've been there. And so have the Old Codger and Son. Now if you were subtle you would see what was going on under your nose, and do something about it.'

'I think we should end this conversation,' said Pentecost, huffily. 'I will only repeat that everything on Lickey Top is under control. And what is more, I can-

13

not see the harm in the Old Codger wishing to end his days in the land of his birth.'

'But Owl can,' Fox pointed out. 'And there lies the rub. For though he is a subtle bird he's out on his back. Until he gets back on his feet you are supposed to be in charge. So why are those small mice running wild? And why is that old nuisance Uncle of yours marching up and down, and issuing ridiculous orders? I can hear him from here.'

'There you go again,' flashed Pentecost. 'For the last time don't tell me how to conduct harvest mouse affairs.'

'Sound advice being the last thing you require?' said Fox with a sigh.

'Precisely,' said Pentecost. Believing the score to be even he relaxed somewhat, and thoughtfully studied the clouds once more.

'Fancy composing a poem?' asked Fox, suddenly. 'It would help pass the time. You can think of a title, and I will do the difficult bits. The linking up of the lines and the like. There you see, we have half a poem already.'

That, fumed Pentecost, was another un-called-for remark. Fox was far and away the better poet, and both knew it. Fox seemed determined to rub this fact in. The mouse thought that Fox was becoming much too personal these days, which meant he was going the right way to be soundly snubbed. But Pentecost decided to ignore the hurtful words of his so-called friend. He would express his distaste with silence. But instead of looking miserable and sorry, Fox, who quite enjoyed golden silences, comfortably settled to wait out the mouse's black mood. He wore on his face that wickedly-kind smile of his, as he studied the back of the other's stiff neck.

Throughout all this Pentecost was trying to think of ways to make Fox change his mind about taking him along on his next adventure. He knew his friend was about to embark on one for two reasons. Number one, because he had been told so by a certain insect, and number two, because he was at this moment looking at that very evidence. Fox's toes were twitching, a dead give-away. It was common knowledge that when Fox was about to make a dangerous tilt at the world, his toes, though never his head, took fright. Now jealousy filled the heart of the mouse. Anger, too. For while Fox had been trying to persuade Pentecost to stay home, he himself was busily planning to shake the dust of the Lickey Hills from his heels. It was too much, and Pentecost made no bones about his feelings as he spoke.

'You lecture me about responsibility?' he said, angrily. 'So why don't you set an example and stay home yourself? I know your game, Fox. While I am carrying out hum-drum tasks on Lickey Top, you will be enjoying yourself in the city. While I am organising boring food-gathering duties, and settling petty squabbles, you will be rummaging in the city dust-bins. And don't deny it, for I can see your toes twitching.'

'My toes are none of your concern,' snapped Fox, bounding to his feet, his temper roused. 'And now get ready, for I intend to ask you some direct questions.'

'Ask away,' replied Pentecost, pleased to note he had Fox on the hop. 'That is, if you can contain your temper. Or do I mean peevishness. . .?'

'Who am I?' demanded Fox. 'Quickly now, no shilly-shallying.'

Pentecost looked confused. 'Why, Fox of .Furrowfield, of course: Surely you haven't forgotten?'

'And what am I?' the other continued, fixing the

mouse with a grilling stare. 'I mean personality-wise.'

'Very subtle for a start,' considered Pentecost. He thought awhile, counting off various points on his paws. 'Also extremely brave, not easily fooled, and very touchy too, I'm just beginning to find out. Why do you ask?'

'Because you are becoming much too familiar and impudent,' Fox retorted. 'And I won't put up with it, do you hear? I am prepared to put up with your moaning and groaning, but I will not tolerate back-chat from scrappy little mice like you. Where I go is my business. I certainly don't have to account for my movements to the likes of you.'

'But you like to keep account of mine,' flared Pentecost. 'Some friend you are!'

'Not another word, do you understand?' thundered Fox. 'I warn you, my patience is wearing thin. If you persist, I will end our friendship here and now, much as I'd hate to.'

Pentecost drooped miserably. He could see that Fox was in deadly earnest. His eyes remained sullenly downcast as more sharp words were heaped upon him.

'So what of this nonsense—theory about twitching toes?' questioned Fox.

'Your toes are no concern of mine,' came the reluctant reply.

'And my supposed trip to the city?'

'A figment of my wild imagination,' sighed the crestfallen mouse.

Fox appeared satisfied. 'So what shall we talk about, bearing in mind what we've just agreed?'

'Dustbins,' said the once-more rebellious mouse, as quick as a flash. He waited for a wrathful storm to break, and felt almost disappointed when it did not.

Instead, another long silence followed. This time it was Fox who stared moodily at the scudding clouds. For his part, Pentecost stared stubbornly into space. It was Fox who finally broke that icy spell. He appeared to be speaking to himself as he voiced certain thoughts.

'Someone has been putting ideas into his head,' he remarked, 'and I've a good idea who that someone is. Filling his head with dreams of wild adventure, indeed . . . .' He then went on to name the culprit. 'That stirring bug has a lot to answer for. One of these days he will come a cropper, and I dearly hope I'm around when he does. That I wouldn's miss for the world. . . .'

'Getting personal, aren't we?' came an angry shout. A lone and innocent-looking foxglove suddenly blazed with an orange light. Surprised, Pentecost and Fox turned to see. There, perched on the flower lip was the rare, seven-legged, orange-backed cockle-snorkle, Owl's companion and private spy. It seemed the bug had listened in on every word; naturally so, for to see and hear all was the name of his game.

'You're right there,' sighed Pentecost. 'But he won't allow anyone else to be personal. It's most frustrating. He seems to have a mental block as far as he and the city are concerned.'

An angry Fox, realising that a long discussion about his failings was about to take place, shut himself off. He went to sleep, or pretended to, in that half-cocked style of his, one eye and an ear ever vigilant. He was wishing now he had stayed down in the Lowlands. He began to make silent vows. . . .

'I mean,' the bug was complaining, 'I don't mind being accused of spying, but if one day I come a cropper, I don't fancy it being turned into a public peepshow. I will treat Fox's remark with the contempt it deserves. And now he's been put in his place, how goes the secret longings, small mouse? Results nil, I take it?'

'What news from the Owl front?' asked Pentecost, anxious to change the subject. Inside he felt vexed and annoyed. It seemed everyone knew about his secret longings. He rushed on, his tone sympathetic. 'Is his nail showing signs of clearing up? Losing one's grip must come as a terrible shock. Is he still mouthing threats at the Old Codger and Son?'

'I am not at liberty to discuss my master's condition,' was the firm reply. 'As a matter of fact I have been sent here to find out the answers to two questions. Firstly, why do you insist upon cluttering up the skyline day after day? Not only are you spoiling the view from Owl's sick-bed, but the sight of the back of your scrawny neck is giving him the pip. Secondly, why haven't you chased that gifted layabout and Son back into the cruel world where they belong? While Owl is out of action, you are supposed to be in charge of his pretty scenic property. So why is Lickey Top beginning to look like a mud-wallow? What have you to say for yourself?'

'For the first part I like to be alone with my thoughts,' replied Pentecost, quietly. 'I'm sorry if my neck annoys Owl, but gazing at the clouds as I do . . . .'

'And question number two?' said the bug, cutting him short, and glowing fiercely.

'The Old Codger and Son are doing no harm, to my mind,' replied Pentecost, more spiritedly. 'What harm is a little churned-up mud? The old one's request to end his days here seems reasonable enough to me.'

'I hope you don't expect Owl to become reasonable.' The bug looked shocked. 'How would you like to be told in advance that your toe-nail was about to turn up?

How do you expect my master to feel? In my opinion, if one has a gift it should be used kindly. Certainly not hurled venomously from the safety of the Weasel Woods.'

'Owl is a fine one to complain,' the mouse retorted. 'Heaven knows, he isn't the kindest of birds. But anyway, none of this interests me. I have enough problems of my own. I just wish to be left in peace.'

'I never thought I'd meet a selfish Pentecost mouse,' mused the bug. 'But really, all this sympathy for the Old Codger and Son is misplaced. I have sussed out their little game. I suppose you know this is the height of the snail season? Take it from me, as soon as they've stripped this place bare they'll trundle away as merry as larks. And leaving behind, I might add, an unholy mess and fleas to boot. But I forget, you have turned your back on all responsibility. And I am totally with you. Look after number one, that's my motto.'

His words stung the mouse as they were meant to. 'What's wrong with having hopes and dreams of one's own?' shouted Pentecost.

'Nothing,' was the flippant reply. 'And what is more, I intend to help you realise those dreams. Together we will sort out all your problems. I gather you tried to get Fox to talk about his adventures in the city? And he took the needle? Well, we won't let that upset us. It so happens I know the city intimately. Business takes me there often, you'll understand. It's my belief an adventurous mouse like yourself would love it there. Now then, when would you be ready to travel?'

'Stop!' cried Pentecost. 'Much as I'd like to see the world, I have my family to consider. I couldn't possibly leave them. A Pentecost mouse wouldn't dream of such a thing.'

'But you do dream about it,' interrupted the bug.

'And as for considering your family, I don't see mu~... evidence of it.' But his banter was short-lived. He was noticing the concern on Pentecost's face. For one brief moment it seemed the leader mouse had been jolted from his self-pitying mood. For a second or two the observant bug saw the old Pentecost, or rather the qualities of that mourned one in the countenance of the other. But the mood-change was brief, and just as quickly gone. Once again Pentecost was his usual miserable and discontented self, with a long, long way to go before he found himself. Much relieved, the bug hastened the weaving of his plot, for as always he had one simmering and thickening.

'I can't understand why a get-up-and-go mouse like you stands for this peaceful life,' he said, his head cocked to one side as he studied the other. 'You'd have a ball in the city, I just know it. If you are worrying about leaving your family for a short time, forget it. They are living on cloud nine these days. They would hardly notice you'd gone. I'm sure they'd jog along quite happily until your return. Remember, you are a derring-do mouse, and need adventure to stretch the mind.'

'I know,' agreed Pentecost, sighing again. 'But I feel so torn. It's my sense of duty, you see. What if I did go to the city, and something terrible happened on Lickey Top while I was away?'

'Think of the future,' urged the bug. 'Just imagine setting out a complete wash-out, and returning a genuine hero, you lucky mouse. Then no one would dare to compare you with the old heroic Pentecost. All your secret longings would come to pass in a mere twinkling of an eye, for you could be there and back from the city in no time at all.'

'I must admit I have a great yearning for adventure,'

Pentecost confessed. 'So far I've done so little with my life. I feel the need to prove myself somehow. And the family don't really need me. They only wish to laze about, re-telling stories about the bravery of the old Pentecost. I sometimes feel I don't exist in their eyes. It is he all the time.'

'And deep down you feel you aren't a patch on him?' sympathised the smoothie insect. 'In short, you think yourself a dyed-in-the-wool failure?'

Pentacost winced. 'I wouldn't put it so strongly, but yes, he did have a mission in life. I was hoping Fox would take me to the city to gain experience, but you heard what happened?'

'Nearly bit your head off,' agreed the bug. 'And now you feel chockered? And so would I if I were the least bit sensitive. That one enjoys playing the heavy fox bit, I'm afraid.' Snug in his foxglove he studied the chockered mouse. He could see how deeply Fox's snub had hurt. He also noticed how from time to time Pentecost's eyes would wander to that neatly-tended mound beneath Owl's tree; to the grave of that hero in whose shadow he lived. But that pensive moment was interrupted by yet more visitors. The bug had been aware of their presence for some time. He proceeded to flush them out in his own malicious fashion.

'It's deplorable that Fox should so cruelly show you up,' he said. 'And in public, too. But I promise this humiliation will go no further. I'm sure the old mouse and his gifted friends will second this. They might even found The Order of the Sealed Snout.'

Pentecost's heart sank. He should have known. Angrily he cast about for Uncle's hiding place. It was then he started with surprise. Before his very eyes where once had been smooth hillock, was now smooth hillock

21

with bumps attached. One large, one small, they were festooned with crushed flowers and grasses, and appeared to be moving slightly.

Presently, from behind the larger bump, a greying head emerged, and Uncle limped forth. 'I was looking for Furrowfield,' he explained, unconvincingly. 'I've searched everywhere, but I can't find him. Oh there he is, and dead too, by the look of it. Pity I'm too late, for I had a very important question to ask him.' With a great deal of puffing, he sank into the grass beside Pentecost, and eyed his leader with a 'call me a liar' expression.

'Great stuff,' giggled the bug. 'I'll bet the Son coached him to say that in the event they were discovered. Uncle has become a puppet to the Son's persuasive powers.'

His words sped like barbed darts to their target. Immediately the young hedgehog became very angry indeed. His quills rattled, and he seemed to swell to twice his normal size. 'How dare you suggest I have the gift of the gab,' he spluttered. 'I am my father's ordinary son, and completely without talent. Have you no respect at all? It so happens we have been scouting for a suitable bit of burying ground, and this particular spot tickled the Old Codger's fancy. You of all people dare accuse me of spying? Take back your wicked slur.'

'I'll do no such thing,' replied the bug, unperturbed by this outburst. 'And don't get stroppy with me. A suitable bit of burying ground, indeed. That old rat-bag will out-live us all. Deny he broke all records haring round Spaghetti Junction to get here.'

'That is a downright lie,' shouted the enraged Son. 'This could well be my dad's last lunch on earth. Do you feel no pity at all?'

'I am as hard and as cold as ice,' replied the bug with pride. 'Indeed, I have never even felt pity for myself.'

'Well, I feel pity,' said Uncle, stoutly. 'I have vowed to help bury the Old Codger the moment he keels over onto his side. My job will be to scrabble out the deep trench.'

The Son was speaking again, but calmer now. 'What of the Pentecost mouse? Is he also in league against us? That would be a pity, for only moments ago my dad's gift was prophesying how adventurous that mouse's future seems. The Old Codger was prepared to put his gift at that mouse's disposal, but he fears he would only get a subtle remark for his pains. . . .'

'That's not true,' protested Pentecost. 'I feel nothing but sympathy for your father.'

'And you truly believe he has the precious gift?' questioned the Son.

'Owl's nail turned up on cue,' replied Pentecost. 'That's proof enough for me.'

'And my father's state of health? Can you see him living to a ripe old age?'

'I will be most surprised if he lasts out the day,' was Pentecost's firm opinion.

'My thoughts exactly,' said the Son, apparently satisfied. 'And because we are in agreement, I am going to press my dad's gift to reveal more of your swashbuckling future.' He craned an ear to the placidly grinding jaws of the old hedgehog. He appeared to be absorbing information, judging by his nods and headshakes. Pentecost, for one, could hear nothing, save for the sickening crunch of snail-shells, but obviously the Son could.

At last the young hedgehog straightened. 'My dad's gift says, the Pentecost mouse will journey to a distant place. There he will meet with one whose destiny it is to overthrow a wicked tyrant, and restore true democracy to his sorely-tried family. The gift sees this all happening in the city. But there will be much confusion, and much unhappiness before God's will prevails. Many trials await the Pentecost mouse and his city soul-mate.

Though their destinies are intertwined, yet they will not at first recognise their twinned fate. The gift sees a large red shape that will play an important role in all this . . . but now the gift fades, for the Old Codger keeps having sinking spells. He says everything has gone suddenly hazy. He reckons his legs will be the next to go.'

'The large red shape being Furrowfield,' guessed Uncle. 'And suddenly hazy because he's kicked the bucket.'

'Fox is merely asleep,' snapped Pentecost, feeling

24

both troubled and elated. 'And he prefers to be addressed as Fox, if you don't mind.'

'If he were merely snoozing there would be steam coming from his nose,' argued Uncle. 'And sharp whistling, as likely as not.'

Somehow Pentecost managed to hold his temper in check. He knew the old mouse was trying to bait him. Uncle was always hanging about in the hope he might make his young leader appear foolish. For all his life Uncle had yearned to be acclaimed as Pentecost and leader. Always this dream had been denied him, for his natural stupidity ruled him out whenever that high office fell vacant. This accounted for his annoying habits, and self-important strutting. And at the moment Uncle was feeling especially jealous that Pentecost's future was being discussed, and not his own. As for Pentecost himself, his thoughts swung between jubilation and despair. For much as he desired an adventure, nevertheless he knew that for a leader to up and leave his family was unthinkable. His place was on Lickey Top. To even consider his own selfish impulses was to flout the complete trust the family held for a Pentecost mouse. And yet . . . .

'Now hold on a minute,' the bug was all indignant. 'I myself am sorting out this mouse's future. And I don't need help, thank you. So if our merry burying party wouldn't mind moving on? Now then, young mouse, we were slanging Fox, were we not?'

'Do you seriously believe you can compete with my dad's gift?' asked the Son, loftily. He lowered his spiky bulk into the grass, and stared at the bug through thickly-lashed eyes. The bug returned his gaze unflinchingly. Instantly, each recognised in the other a bitter enemy. Throughout all this the Old Codger remained busy, crunching and munching, and poking about in search of those whirly-shelled snails he was so fond it. For one so gifted he seemed amazingly uninterested in the argument. Indeed, at times he appeared not to know where he was. Often, between mouthfuls, he would squint about him, a blank expression in his eyes, only to shake his head in bewilderment. Immediately he would return to the task in hand, namely lunch. For there was no doubting his understanding of that. Contentedly he browsed on, uttering small grunts of pleasure at each new find, his jaws grinding rythmically without cease.

'Quiet,' hissed the Son. 'There's more coming through.' Once again he took up his listening post, his face set and grave. 'What's that, Dad? You see a mouse returning from the city . . . but he will not be what he seems . . . and he will be the cause of great . . . ' Sorry, the gift has gone haywire again.'

'I have a question to ask of the oh, so brave Pentecost mouse,' said the pensive-eyed bug. 'It concerns the city, and it is this: how would you react if I told you that city mice are the hardest, roughest, cruellest bunch of scoundrels on the face of God's earth? And that if you so much as set a paw inside the city, they'd throw you to Black Shadow before you had time to open your mouth? Take it from me, a close encounter with Black Shadow would be no picnic. Summed up it is this: would you still brave the city even though I've just scared you out of your wits?'

'I would face this Black Shadow squarely,' replied Pentecost, his heart giving a little flip of fear. 'But first of all I would make friends with the city mice. I would learn their ways, and try to understand them. I would not flinch from danger, Cockle-snorkle. But all this questioning is silly. I've told you I'm not going.'

26

The Old Codger raised his head from the grass. Suddenly revealed was a moist snout, two coal-black eyes, and a set of muddy whiskers. The eyes blinked as a pink mouth yawned dozily, lips smacking as if to taste the scented air. With a huge sigh he lumbered off, Uncle, bored out of his mind by the question and answer game, limping along behind. The Son remained, stubby nose held high as he regarded Pentecost and the bug in snooty silence.

'Forget something?' asked the bug. 'Waiting for the last of our itchy friends to climb aboard, are we? There's kindness.'

'Insult me all you wish,' replied the Son. 'But you are wasting your time. I have suffered every cruel and subtle remark the world could heap upon me. I have been harried from one end of the earth to the other. Every curse I have endured, and in many tongues. Now I am come home to the land of my birth, here to die in peace. It was my misfortune to be born with 'the gift', and for that I have paid more than full measure. The fear and suspicion my presence creates wearies me. I wish only to end my days amidst the kindness of understanding friends.'

'Now let's get this straight,' said the puzzled bug. 'I always thought it was the Old Codger who was born with the gift. Do you mean to say it was you who turned Owl's toe-nail up?'

'The words I speak are my father's,' replied the Son. 'It has ever been my fate to live in his shadow. I am merely his mouthpiece and protector. I was born to have nothing to say on my own behalf. And now, the reason why I stayed behind. My dad wishes the small Pentecost mouse every success as he embarks upon his mission. He warns him to expect to meet much heart-

27

ache, and many dangers in the city. But as to whether things will turn out right in the end, my dad cannot say. Already his gift gets hazier by the minute, and he doubts if he will live to enjoy supper-time. So if he does not see you again, he bids you farewell, and good luck on your venture, for you are an unsubtle mouse, and thus his friend.' So saying he turned to depart, his quills now in accord with his evened temper, flat along his back.

'Makes you think, doesn't it?' said the bug, breaking the silence, and eyeing the confused mouse. 'So when do you plan to set out? No time like the present, I say. By the way, have you noticed, your toes are twitching. First Fox's, now yours. I wonder what that can mean?'

Bewildered, Pentecost glanced down. The bug spoke true. It was as if those squirming objects were no longer part of him. They seemed eager and impatient to be off and away. The same could not be said for their owner. The dreamer, the would-be hero mouse was filled with fear and doubt. Yet somewhere, deep down in his soul, Pentecost knew he must go to the city. He pondered the words of the Old Codger . . . the Pentecost mouse will journey to a distant place . . . he will meet one whose destiny is to overthrow a wicked tyrant . . . they will not at first recognise their twinned fate . . . a large red shape will play an important role in all this. . . . And then suddenly Pentecost no longer doubted. Every fibre in his being was now urging go, go. All thought for his trusting family was swept from his mind. Their welfare no longer seemed important. No more was he that discontented mouse, destined to sit upon a hill, ever-dwelling in the shadow of a hero. At last he had a mission in life, and everything else paled into insignificance. Now the twitching of his toes spread swiftly throughout his body. He leapt to his paws, eager and ready to tackle the great task that lay before him. It was at that moment that Fox awoke with a start. Rising and stretching, he glanced at the sun. It was beginning to set.

'Nice to know death isn't a permanent thing, eh Fox?' this from the impish bug. He went on. 'By the way, you'll be pleased to know you will have company on your journey to the city tonight.'

'I'm ready whenever you are, Fox,' said an excited Pentecost. 'Would you allow me a few moments to explain things to the family? About my mission, I mean?'

'What's he on about?' growled Fox. Then he remembered that he and the mouse had fallen out. Hastily he muttered something about having to get away.

'Just a few seconds,' pleaded the mouse. 'I'm sure I can make the family understand the heroic nature of my mission. They will soon realise I am not deserting them. After all, didn't the Old Codger say I will return, the cause of great . . . it must mean rejoicing, Fox?'

'You can have all the seconds in the world,' snapped Fox, unkindly. 'For if you mean what I think you mean, you can forget it. Get it into your head, I travel alone.'

'But you don't understand,' cried Pentecost, despairingly. 'You and I are destined to brave the perils of the city together. The Old Codger foretold it.'

'Which goes to show how little he knows,' retorted Fox, the rebuff delivered curtly over a shoulder, as he sloped away. He didn't look back again.

'Surely you don't still bear a grudge,' yelled Pentecost. There was no reply. Fox was already at the bottom of the hill and entering the woods.

'We have upset him,' remarked the bug. 'Or rather, you have. Now what?' Pentecost was drooping miserably, and not for the first time. Fox had again knocked

29

the stuffing out of him. 'Cheer up,' said the bug. 'Have faith in the Old Codger's gift. If he says you and Fox share this mission, so it will be. Perhaps fate intends to re-unite you at some later time? Down in the Lowlands, maybe? So come on, show a leg. Time and foxes wait for no mouse. Best paw forward, and all that . . . .'

Deep down he felt a flicker of sympathy for the fate-torn mouse. Up top he felt none at all. Strange, mused the bug, how sometimes I could almost swear I feel emotion. I wonder what it actually feels like to truly care? But then the voice of the mouse was interrupting his reverie. The other was muttering to himself. 'If I ran all the way . . . he couldn't force me to turn back . . . it's a free world after all . . . anyway, fated missions can never be thwarted, not even by foxes who have caught the hump. . . .'

'He has a good head start,' urged the bug. 'I wouldn't delay any longer. You can pick up his trail the other side of Furrowfields. It's my guess he'll nip home first. If you lie in wait beside the trail that leads to the city until he comes bowling along . . . hey. . .!'

Pentecost was already scurrying down the hill. A few mice watched him race by, but they soon returned to their gathering of supper. There was nothing unusual about Pentecost wandering alone in the Weasel Woods. They knew he had much on his mind these days and liked to be alone with his thoughts. The possibility that he might not return never occurred to them, and why should it? They knew nothing of their leader's destined mission in the city. Only the cockle-snorkle knew that and he would only tell them when he thought the time to be ripe. The bug had long been bored with the peace and tranquillity on Lickey Top. The departure of the Pentecost mouse would change all that. Oh, what joy to be the bearer of bad news, smiled the bug, for he surely would be. He knew he could rely on Uncle to have forgotten the discussion that had taken place a short time ago. The harvest mice would be sleeping peacefully, innocently unaware that their leader had up and gone. For the bug the stage was set. . . .

Tumbling, stumbling, Pentecost picked his way through the dark trees. Soon he had emerged from the other side of the wood, and was hurrying across the smooth Plateau for the One Hundred Steps. Down he went, head over heels, bruised and sore even at this early stage of the journey. But he seemed not to care. He was a mouse obsessed. Never once did he pause to consider his responsibilities as leader. All he could think of was the excitment of new horizons, and a triumphant home-coming. For only then would he be able to gaze upon that flower-strewn mound unashamedly, only then could he step from the shadow of that hero who haunted his life. This was his simple and foolish reasoning.

The sun had gone. Pentecost shivered and scurried on. Soon, thankfully, he was tripping over the roughly-ploughed earth of Furrowfields. A quick search and he had found the trail that meandered alongside. One questing sniff told him all he wished to know. This was Fox's personal path to the city. He settled down to wait. His confidence was high. Quite soon a once close friend would be passing by. . . .

High on Lickey Top a small bug glowed bright. For some time the plotting insect had clung to the lip of his foxglove, listening to the exciting sounds of the night. A loud crunching caused him to smile wryly. Not far away the Old Codger, having survived the going down of the sun, was enjoying a moonlit supper. Beside him the Son was whispering words of encouragement, and praying that the dawn would not find him all alone in this cruel world.

'What fun,' murmured the bug to himself. His smile became a grimace as he began to rehearse a little. 'I regret to inform you that your leader has deserted Lickey Top. As the oldest and wisest mouse, you must be prepared to shoulder many heavy burdens in the days ahead. But you can rely on me to help you all I can. In the meantime keep this to yourself, for it would be heartless to disturb the family at this time. I intend to chase after that wayward mouse in the hope that I can persuade him to return. But if I fail, you will have to break the shocking news, first thing in the morning. . . . But pray, toes crossed, it doesn't come to that.'

His glow was now at full power as he spread tiny wings. Soon he was zooming down towards the untidy, grass-spun home of an old mouse called Uncle. 'Deeply shocked,' he muttered. His expression was one of tragic doom. But still he smiled, inside. . . .

2 A Crawl of Bright Light

His toes were firm upon the path as he trotted along. No twitching now, Fox was in complete control of body and mind. He had shrugged off the nagging doubts that always troubled him before a risky venture. Before leaving, he had looked in on his mate and cubs. They were safe and well. Thus contented, he was able to enjoy the journey. There on the moonlit path, with great ceremony, he gave his tail a good old chasing.

Yet for all his contentment, Fox couldn't quite shake off a feeling of annoyance. The events of the afternoon had bruised his pride. He had been slanged by the detestable bug, dismissed as dead by an old grey mouse, and cross-examined by Pentecost. At least, that mouse had attempted it. And the mighty Furrowfield's reply to these insults? He had feigned sleep until true drowsiness had finally overcome him, and on awakening, had slunk away, his self-respect in tatters. It was the end, of course. He would stay clear of Lickey Top in future. He made a silent vow that from this day forth he would stick to his Lowland home, and the Pentecost mouse could go hang. He would become again the loner fox as God intended. And the hurts and hopes of others? None of his concern. It was surprising how much better he felt to have thrashed that matter out in his mind.

Suddenly his thoughts, for a while so far away, returned to here and now. Instantly he was all stealth and cocked-ears, and for good reason. He was listening to the soft patter of paws just behind. Then the realisation dawned. He, Fox of Furrowfield, was being followed. At first he could scarcely believe the evidence of his ears. Who on earth would have the gall, the sheer incredible nerve, to stalk the most famous stalker in the Midlands? And for what reason? Well, he would soon find out. Softly he stole into a bush beside the path, and waited. Now the whispered footfalls were very near. Someone was in a lathered haste judging by the harsh and laboured breathing. As the stranger drew level, so Fox pounced. In a flash his splayed paw had trapped a small, wriggling form. Muffled yells came from beneath the mound of crackling leaves swept up in the capture. Ignoring them, Fox began carefully to unveil his prey. It was then his curiosity turned to anger. One glance at those floppy ears, the startled eyes, was recognition enough. Fox released the mouse, sat back upon his haunches, and waited for an extremely good explanation.

'Don't do anything rash, Fox,' said Pentecost, brushing himself down with shaking paws. In the meantime he nervously studied the other's angry expression. The mouse rushed on to explain. 'I truly meant to stay home on Lickey Top, honest I did. But then fate intervened. While you were asleep the Old Codger looked into my future and prophesied that I would go to the city on a vital mission. That was what I tried to tell you on Lickey Top, but you loped off in a huff. If you will listen to the details you will realise that this mission is bigger than both of us, Fox. But I expect you are anxious to hear about your important role in all this. You'll be pleased to learn that fate has a soft spot for you, Fox, for you are warmly referred to as "a large red shape". . . .'

Quickly, Pentecost related the strange prophecy as foretold by the Old Codger and Son. Fox listened quietly, though looking very sceptical indeed. Afterwards it was the mouse's turn to fall silent as he waited for Fox's reaction. It came swiftly. 'Mice who make up stories come to sticky ends,' warned Fox. Then in slow and measured tones, 'I am not going to call you a liar, I am simply going to ask you to turn around and go home.'

Pentecost was suddenly defiant. 'So this is the crunch, then? I was right all along. You have always looked down your long nose at me. Now you accuse me of making up stories. Well, Fox, a placid and boring

34

mouse you might think me, but a liar I have never been. Take back that slur on my character, or face the consequences. I may not win the battle, but I choose death before dishonour. So begin your grisly work! I will never turn back.'

'Very well,' said Fox, grimly. 'I will give you the benefit of the doubt. I will try to accept your incredible story. As for taking back that slur on your character, I will do better than that.'

'You will?' said Pentecost, surprised. This was better than he had hoped. Inside he was glorying in a battle won.

'Indeed,' replied Fox, shortly. 'As you are not only hell-bent, but . . . you did say fated . . . to go to the city, I intend to see you arrive there.'

'You see?' cried Pentecost triumphantly. 'Even you can't fight destiny. You are even now clicking helplessly into your role as "the large red shape". How does it feel to be no longer your own master, Fox?'

'That day will never dawn,' was the reply. 'But speaking of masters I hope the pupil is prepared, for you are about to be taught a lesson you may not live to regret.'

'I am quite prepared,' said Pentecost, raising a proud head. 'But don't be surprised if I earn full marks, for I was always good at lessons, Fox.'

'And what of your family while you are gallivanting about the city?' questioned Fox. 'Have you spared a thought for them? Who is in charge up there in the meantime? I only know the old Pentecost would never have deserted his post to satisfy his own selfish yearnings for adventure.'

'The family don't need me,' replied Pentecost, looking downcast. 'I doubt if they will ever notice I've gone. But things will be different when I return, for I am certain that fate has chosen me for this mission that I might prove myself in their eyes. Then it will be my exploits that are talked about instead of. . . . ' His voice trailed away.

'Yes,' said Fox hurriedly. 'But let's keep our feet on the ground for the moment, eh? First things first. For instance there are a few things you should know about the city. Supposing . . . and only supposing what the Old Codger said is true, then we must approach this project sensibly. You would be making a grave mistake if you ventured into the city with stars in your eyes.'

'Not a lecture?' groaned Pentecost, impatiently.

'Yes, a lecture,' snapped Fox, his eyes flashing. 'And you will listen. First of all, get it into your head, you won't be welcome where we're going. And have you considered how huge the city is? So how are you supposed to find this so-called "twin-soul" mouse of yours? You could search for ever, especially when, as the Old Codger informed you, you won't at first even recognise the little scruff.'

'You don't go much on divine destinies, do you, Fox?' said Pentecost, in a peeved voice. 'You much prefer to scoff your way through life.'

'Not at all,' returned Fox. 'I'm just being practical. But I realise there's no changing your stubborn mind, so I'll prepare you for what you are soon to see. For instance, the meanness, the hopelessness, and the hunger. You will see the city-mice going about their miserable business, and feel smug that you have never had to sink so low. You will witness blackmail, treachery, and yes, maybe murder. But only if you're lucky, for a soft country mouse like you would make a perfect victim. What I'm afraid of is you waltzing up to the first city mouse you meet and cheerfully saying you have been

36

sent to make his life all sweetness and light. I know exactly what his answer will be. He will smile and say, "thank you very much", and tear you apart for the sheer hell of it. Let me tell you, silly mouse, heroes don't go to the city, they live there. For one needs to be a hero to endure such an existence. So do you still want to go?'

'You won't put me off, Fox,' replied Pentecost, breezily. 'Anyway, if it's so awful there, how come you are so eager to go?'

'There is a certain word,' said Fox, quietly. 'It's called "risk". My nature being what it is, there are times in my life when I feel the urge to gamble against odds. But you could never understand. So are you ready to travel?' He said no more. Turning, he set off along the trail.

'Wait,' cried Pentecost. 'You surely don't expect me to keep up with you? You do intend to bound along as fast as the wind?'

'If not faster,' replied an irritated Fox, pausing and looking back. 'I aim to be there by midnight.'

'With your stride, maybe,' Pentecost said. 'But the measure of mine could spell days.'

'I don't care for the way this conversation is going,' grimaced Fox, guessing what the mouse had in mind.

'I was thinking if you lowered your nose to the trail, I could climb aboard, take a firm hold on your ears, and if you really stretched your legs we'd both arrive about the time you specify?'

Fox thought the idea undignified, but he reluctantly consented. The mouse climbed aboard. They crossed the Great River by way of an old stone bridge. Not a keen swimmer, Fox thought it well worth the extra mile's lope downstream to reach it. Then it was a quick dash over, hugging the wall, their eyes dazzled by the headlights of the traffic leaving the city. Soon the Lickey

37

Hills were far behind, and they were travelling through country increasingly dotted with the lights from the sprawling housing estates. Sometimes the trail would end abruptly, its progress barred by yet another new fence-line. Wearily, Fox could only detour, dreading the day when even that would prove impossible. Now they were crossing quiet lanes, their smutty lamp-posts casting pools of feeble light upon the weed-choked kerbs. On either side were unkempt privet hedges, affording cover for the now stealthy pair. Suddenly Fox stopped. For a while he sniffed the air, one paw upraised and quivering. Then he was diving into an evil-smelling ditch, was slipping along it, the mouse clinging on tight, soaked and shivering, his fur now thick with mud. Again Fox paused. Once more the air was tested. Then a quick leaping and twisting movement, and he was a-top an old brick wall, was squeezing through the iron railings into the park beyond. Once inside, no words were exchanged as Fox slumped down to rest, his eyes ever scanning the night. At last Pentecost could relax his grip, and with much relief, flex stiff paws.

It was near midnight, the park deserted. Quietly sitting upon the close-mown turf, the pair watched the lights in the encircling houses wink out, one by one. Soon Fox's attention switched. He raised his head to gaze intently at the gently rising slope, just beyond a small boating lake. There the sky-line was tinged with a strange and pulsating glow. Still without speaking, Fox snapped to his feet and was off, the speed of it all almost flinging the mouse from his precarious perch. In no time they had circled the lake, Fox pausing not once until he had reached the crest of the slope. And there he lay down, to stare out over the view below. No matter how many times he came here, the sight never ceased to enthrall him. Pentecost, seeing it for the first time, was also enraptured. For as far as the eye could see sprawled a crawl of bright light. Multi-coloured, it resembled the web of a monstrous spider, the beast itself a sparkling jewel at its hub.

'There's your city,' said Fox, breaking the spell. 'I suppose you would say it was beautiful? But then so are many evil things. Come, and may you never regret this night.'

At the bottom of the hill, a wide expanse, black and deserted, barred their way. Spaced out along either side were tall, tulip-like columns, each beaming a violet light down on that dark, mirroring surface. Just then the silence was shattered as a huge swaying shape came careering past, its baleful eyes illuminating the crouching pair. Cautiously, Pentecost opened his eyes, uncovered his ringing ears. Valiantly, he fought a rising fear. Already he was beginning to regret this venture. Yet deep down he knew there was no turning back. His destiny, whatever horrors it held, lay somewhere in that teeming city beyond.

'Having second thoughts?' asked Fox, reading the mouse's face. He didn't wait for a reply. Quickly, he padded across that slick surface and scrambled through matted greenery, before continuing at a wary trot the journey into the city proper.

At Fox's prompting, the mouse slid to the ground and began to follow his friend through the dingy streets. Hugging the slimy walls, freezing at every sound, Pentecost became quickly stripped of all romantic notions. Grass, wild-flowers, a broad open sky, things he had so taken for granted, all were absent from this grim place. Dark and threatening, the city had long ago broken and devoured all that challenged it. Beauty gained no hold here. The grey of featureless concrete reigned supreme. And all about lurked an air of brooding menace.

Pentecost saw his first dustbin down a narrow alley-way. There was a row of them, each it seemed competing to out-smell its neighbour. Wide-eyed, the mouse shrank against the wall as Fox carefully eased the buckled lid from the nearest, just a little way – barely enough to slip a sensitive nose inside. He then proceeded to snuffle and rummage amongst the items within. . . . But Pentecost was no longer watching his friend. Trembling violently, he was listening to two distinct sounds. The first was a furtive scuffling of paws, the second, the thump of his own heart loud in his ears. Now Pentecost, the would-be hero, was quaking against a city wall. That once confident mouse with a mission to help overthrow a tyrant, and thus herald in the new dawn, was at this moment wishing with all his being that he had stayed safe home on Lickey Top. But it was much too late for regrets. Things were happening fast. *Crash*: Fox also aware that they were no longer alone, fumbled and slipped, sending the dustbin-lid clattering to the cobbles of the alley-way. Then the night became rent by a dreadful yowling sound. It seemed to be coming from behind the bins. Wildly, Pentecost cast about, his one thought but to escape. The night-city abruptly exploded into violence as squeals of terror echoed up and down the alley. Bangs and thuds all joined in concert, shaking Pentecost from his frozen state. He made to run, too late. He felt himself swept up, found himself fleeing amidst a tide of frantic mice, all seeking shelter from some unidentified wrath. In the meantime Fox was spinning and snapping about him in bewilderment, as he sought to close with the unseen enemy. For a few seconds he was a lost soul.

But despite the natural concern for his own hide, he still spared a thought for the safety of his friend. And then he spied him – was just in time to catch a glimpse of that familiar brown and white pelt disappearing with a throng of mice, all pouring like a living water-fall through a hole in the alley wall. As he dashed forward to help, so the source of all this fear lashed out at his throat. Cruel, sleek, and green of eye, Black Shadow spat and tore. Slipping and dodging, somehow the hero of Furrowfield broke free. Then as if in a dream he was running, running, knowing not nor caring where his fleeting paws led him.

3 The Gas Street Mob

'Calm yourselves,' rasped a heavily-accented voice. 'Stack the loot, and let's have you back in here.'

Obediently, the band of rascally mice slouched across the cellar, to disappear through a hole in the farther wall. Soon they were trooping back to form a ragged line before their leader. But reluctantly, for their mouths were watering, their eyes still retaining the image of those golden nuggets of cheese.

'That was the sloppiest raid ever.' The leader's angry gaze flicked over the humbled Mob. 'It's a miracle we made it back. So what happened to the Scouts? And what were the Decoys playing at? Talk about slip-shod. By the way, I hope there's been no pilfering?'

One of the mice suddenly choked, a spray of golden

crumbs issuing from his mouth. His eyes bulged as he coughed. His actions were those of a criminal caught in the act. The other mice looked away. At the dripping walls, the coal-dusted floor, anywhere but at their hapless comrade, for they had no wish to become involved. To show compassion could be to share his fate, and life was too precious for that. For the code of the city was clear on this point: 'Do unto others, what you hope they won't do unto you.' True to this rule the Gas Street Mob studiously pretended the accused wasn't there. Thus, the little thief stood quite alone as Zero, his leader, approached him. There was no pity in his eyes.

'You know the penalty?' he snapped. 'Or do you deny stealing precious rations?'

The thief mumbled something, but all that came from his mouth was more evidence of guilt. Annoyed, Zero brushed cheese-crumbs from his moulting black fur. 'He hasn't even the good manners to swallow,' he said, contemptuously. He addressed the fidgeting Mob. 'Will anyone speak in his defence? Not that it will do him much good.'

'Well, I'm his best friend,' offered a sneaky-looking mouse. 'And I can truthfully say he has stolen many times before. Will that cast-iron fact help him, I wonder?'

'So this isn't the first time?' snapped Zero. 'You don't deserve such a loyal friend to stick by you. Have you anything to say for yourself, before I pass sentence?'

The thief gave a large gulp, sucked his teeth, and stuck out his jaw. There was something noble and brave about that last gesture. There were many furtive and sympathetic glances in his direction.

'Damned by his own closed mouth,' said Zero, his eyes glistening evilly. 'An open and shut case, if ever there was. Have you any last words?'

At last the thief-mouse found his voice. 'I just wish to say that the Sneak is no friend of mine,' he retorted. 'Everyone knows he's after my job.'

'Your job being what?' enquired Zero.

'Scout, First Class,' was the proud reply.

'Yet from such a trusted position you stoop to slander?' yelled Zero. 'This is serious indeed. Your friend will deny it, naturally.'

'I certainly do,' said the Sneak, hotly. 'I make no bones about yearning to move up a notch, but then I'm extremely ambitious. You of all mice would understand that, Zero.'

'There is no law against wishing to better oneself,' agreed the leader. 'There is always room at the top for a mouse who would shop his best friend in the interests of the Mob as a whole. What is your post, by the way?'

'Decoy, Third Class,' came the bitter reply. 'And needless to say I don't like it much. Decoys are just set-up patsies. They only have a three week life expectancy. I'm already into my second week, and the days seem to be flashing by. So who wouldn't angle for promotion in my position?'

'Yes, well we all have to start at the bottom,' replied Zero. 'But I take your point.'

'You didn't start at the bottom,' reminded the Sneak, cunningly. 'I'm thinking about your great leap upwards, after your father went down with a mysterious chill on his chest. That poor old ex-leader has never been the same since. . . .'

'We are not here to mull over the past,' snarled Zero, interrupting. Quickly he changed the subject. 'So what do we do with this thieving scout, lads?'

'Take him up by ears and toes,
Swing him twice and out he goes. . .' chanted the Mob.

'A date with Black Shadow is the penalty for grand theft,' roared Zero. 'And why, lads?'

'Because that is the Law,' chorused the mice. But their responses were automatic. It was obvious they were prompted by fear. And they had good reason to be afraid. For grouped around Zero were his three bully-mice. Dim the trio might be, but they were tough and nearly bursting with menace. And extra cheese rations, too – for that was how Zero kept them loyal and sweet.

The leader looked pleased. 'Let this punishment serve as a warning to us all. In those wise words, "Justice was not only done, it was carried out. . . ."'

'Seen to be done,' corrected a reddish-brown mouse

45

with a white chest, and paws to match. He sat alone against the cellar wall. Unlike the other mice he showed no fear at all. He continued. 'I'm sorry, Zero, but I can't abide sloppy quotations. And must you look so cheerful? Thief or not, the Scout is still our brother.'

'Do you think I enjoy this?' Zero shouted.

'I sincerely hope not,' said the other. 'And there's no cause to get niggly. Just because I try to pass on a few leadership tips.'

'Getting ready to take over?' sneered Zero. 'It will be over my dead body. I knew you when you were afraid of your own shadow. All you ever did was weep and cringe. Now you've got a bob on yourself. "Chosen" indeed. All that guff about "wandering in the wilderness". It wouldn't surprise me if you turned out to be a phoney. A mere mouse of straw. You annoy me no end.'

'That's no surprise,' came the lofty reply. 'All tyrants hate Chosen mice. But remember, one day my time will come as yours will pass, for I have a mission in life. When I'm ready to take over I won't let you know. How's that for a taste of your own unfair medicine?'

Zero swallowed hard. There was fear in his eyes. Pea-brained he might be, but he was wise enough not to tempt the fates. The claims of the Chosen mouse could be a pack of lies. But what if they weren't? His mixed feelings were not shared by the rest of the Mob. Simple souls, they had accepted the story with not a little awe. For the mouse's amazing experience had shaken them rigid when he returned from the 'dead' to relate it. . . .

It appeared that a week ago, having foolishly strayed outside the Mob's territory, the mouse had blundered on to that huge human folly known as Spaghetti Junction. Amidst this confusing maze of soaring ramps and roadways, he soon became hopelessly lost. For two days he wandered around and around in dizzying circles. On the third day, just when he had given up hope, the miracle occurred. Out of the smoke and fumes came limping an old hedgehog, his son leading the way. They paused to speak, and after a while the son, speaking on behalf of his father, congratulated the poor lost mouse on his complete lack of subtlety. He remarked that his father had taken a shine to him, and what was more, the mouse was in luck, for his future looked bright indeed. At this point the mouse, tired and hungry, began to weep. He also began to scratch, for the kind strangers were alive with fleas. Thus, his misery complete, he buried his face in his paws, and let it all come out. Sobbing, he told how all his life he had been mocked and bullied – how he had never been able to hold down a job for more than a day or two, and how his despair had caused him to wander so far a field. In short, he ended, he was a hopeless case, and best left to his fate. Tears poured from his grimy eyes as the bitter words burst from him. And the hedgehog and his son were deeply moved. It was then, through the son, that the oldster spoke words that filled the mouse with hope.

'Do not despair,' he was told. 'For you have it in you to become a leader amongst mice. But first you will go on a great journey to a beautiful place, where lunch is plentiful, and the living easy. There you will be cleansed inside and out, that you may be humbled to learn many lessons, for wise is the true leader. A large red shape will play an important role in all this. Go now even with closed eyes, for your destiny beckons, and will guide you safely home. But a word of warning. For a time there will be much confusion, . . . there is another mouse . . . a lost and frightened mouse . . . he is your soul-mate . . . he will suffer until the time when you are fit to return from that beautiful place, to put all things right. You will not at first know him, for neither of you will be what you seem . . . and now the vision becomes hazy . . . I can tell you no more. . . . ' With those last hesitant words, the pair ambled off into the choking smog.

Bewildered, the now Chosen mouse, eyes tightly shut, set off he knew not where. Suddenly light of heart and step, he circled blindly to the north, veered west, swung due east, spun round on the spot a few times, and eventually arrived home safe and sound in the Gas Street cellar.

From that day forth he was a changed mouse. But alas, not for the better. The humbleness he had felt on Spaghetti Junction vanished. Glorying in his status as a Chosen mouse, he soon became over-bearing, boastful and cocky. Gone was the nervous stutter that had plagued him all his life. No longer was he the put-upon mouse of old. In no time at all he was living the life of Riley, and enjoying every moment of it. Now he was feared, for having listened to his creepy tale, the Gas Street Mob thought it wise to cater to his every whim. It was a foolish mouse who dared to pick holes in his story. For what God-fearing mouse would seek to tangle with one so Chosen? The lucky mouse was soon basking in all this attention. He became idle, greedy and selfish. He refused all offers of a secure job, preferring to spend his time lounging about scoffing cheese, while his comrades fetched and carried for him. Indeed, if this was the mouse destined to become a wise and fair leader, someone 'up there' had slipped down badly. In the meantime he just lay about, waiting for act two of his destiny. His attitude was one of boredom. It was as if he was waiting to hear the end of a joke that was becoming tedious. He had indeed a lot to learn . . . .

'I wish I were less subtle, and had got lost on Spaghetti Junction,' said the Sneak, often and enviously. 'How marvellous it must be to have everyone over a barrel. It's so depressing being at the bottom of the heap, with one's life ticking away. Who'd be a Decoy, when one could be a lucky Chosen mouse?'

Alone of all the Mob, Zero remained suspicious. But then he had the most to lose. If the story of the Chosen mouse was true, he could well be overthrown. And what would become of him then? But Zero was a cunning mouse. Not clever, but shifty. He bided his time, waiting for the right moment to dispose of his potential rival. He also made sure that his bully-mice were well-fed, and surly. And all the while he checked and re-checked the story of the Chosen mouse.

'Just you wait,' he would say, threateningly. 'One word of your tale that doesn't tally, and I'll have your guts for garters.'

But the Chosen mouse had put cringing and fear behind him. For answer he would lounge back, toss a crumb of cheese into the air, to catch it deftly in his mouth. . . . He was doing that trick now. 'If I may venture an opinion,' he said, 'I mean about the accused Scout . . . of course, you don't have to take notice of me. . . .'

'His remarks get pithier every day,' gasped the Sneak. 'He knows very well we have to take notice of him, after his lucky break on the motorway.'

Zero silenced him, and addressed his enemy. 'If you are about to plead for the Scout, forget it. His guilt is obvious. As leader of the Mob I am perfectly within my rights to pass sentence.'

The eyes of the Chosen mouse were insolent beneath his strangely drooping ears. 'How about taking a vote on it? he said, coolly. 'But I forgot, you never did learn to count, eh Zero?'

Zero glared. 'And what's that supposed to mean? Don't give me any of that Chosen stuff.'

'It means he's about to make a bid for the leadership,' babbled the Sneak. He shivered with delight, causing the streak of yellow fur down his back to undulate, snake-like. 'He's cleverly saying that your days are numbered, and you can't see it, my leader.'

Zero appeared to cringe a little. Behind his bullying pose lurked a very unsure mouse indeed. For a while he was at a loss for words. The Sneak continued. Crawlingly, he said, 'But you can count on my support if he tries to topple you, Zero. Which brings me to a ticklish question. May I ask it?'

'By all means,' replied the leader, relieved by this show of loyalty.

'Well you know my best friend?' pressed the Sneak. 'The one we are about to Black Shadow for theft?'

'You are not my best friend,' shouted the thief-scout, angrily. 'Your type has no pals. You and I know who is the criminal. Think yourself lucky that a Scout never twits.'

'If you will bear with me a moment,' butted in the Chosen mouse.

Zero glowered. 'The Decoy wishes to ask a question. I'm tired of you hogging all the lime-light. Carry on, Decoy.'

'Well, I'm thinking you'll be needing a replacement Scout before too long,' said the eager Sneak. 'I wish to apply for the post immediately, before some climber beats me to it.'

'Consider yourself newly-promoted,' replied Zero, giving the fawning creature a pat. 'And now lads, all that remains is to Black Shadow the thief. Is he prepared?'

'No, he isn't,' said the Scout, stubbornly. 'But still I will not twit.'

'A Scout cannot tell a lie,' shouted an irate, one-eyed mouse, a second-class Breaker, from the back. 'This case needs probing, if you ask me.'

'But I am an unshakable witness against him,' yelled the desperate Sneak. 'Do you think I like doing this to a pal?'

'*For the last time, you are not my pal*,' snapped the Scout, emphasising each word. 'And I have something else to say. Although I never twit, nevertheless I have the right to ask, did anyone see what really happened? Who amongst you will clear my good name?'

Silence fell over the cellar. No one spoke. The Scout was looking anxiously into the eyes of his comrades. But no one stepped forward. It seemed the incident of the stolen cheese had passed unnoticed. 'There's your answer,' sneered Zero. 'Take hold of him, lads. Carry out the sentence.'

Unwilling paws took hold of the condemned mouse. Much as they hated this, the Mob respected the Law. Sadly, they escorted the prisoner to the hole in the wall. Only Zero, his bullies, and the Sneak seemed eager to get the sordid business over with. The proud Scout remained silent as he was picked up, swung once, swung twice, and was about to be swung for the last time, when a high and clear voice was heard.

'Stop! The Scout, First Class is innocent.'

The Gas Street Mob froze in mid-swing. There followed an eerie and lengthy silence, broken only by the drip, drip of water down the cellar wall. Then suddenly as one, the shaken mice swivelled their heads to stare towards a darkened corner. It was from there the voice had come. Yet all was so still and quiet now. And nothing could be seen, save for an old and broken roof-tile, gathering cobwebs. Afraid, the Mob released the Scout and stood fidgeting. At long last Zero found his voice.

'Okay,' he said, shakily. 'Come out the joker. Come out whoever thinks life in the city's a barrel of laughs. Come out the mouse who fancies being Black Shadowed too.'

'Whoever he is, he's trying to put a spoke in my wheel,' complained the Sneak. 'I feared this all along. I am praying a dangerous witness isn't hiding in that dark corner.'

Then the Chosen mouse was speaking. 'It seems we are one too many,' he remarked, with maddening calmness. He directed his cool glance at Zero. 'So what does our beloved leader plan to do about it?'

'It cannot be,' came a cracked, but vigorous voice. A figure emerged from the hole in the farther wall. An elderly mouse pushed his way through the crush to approach Zero. It was the ex-leader, Zero's father. Since having been overthrown by his son, the excuse being a 'heavy chill on the chest', the old mouse still wished to remain useful. These days he counted the Mob in and out from cheese-raids, for numbers had always fascinated him.

'Speak up, old one.' Unkindly, Zero refrained from addressing him as 'father'. He spoke harshly on: 'I suppose you know this is Mob business. So come on, be quick about it. Say what you have to say, and then get back into the family quarters where you belong.

'I may be stooped and retired, but my eyes are still good,' replied the proud old mouse. 'And I say you cannot be one too many. For I counted you out, and I counted you back in again.'

'And what total did you arrive at?' asked Zero, impatiently. 'So make with the figures.'

The old mouse stood shuffling his paws. 'I forget,' he muttered, miserably. Without another word he retraced his feeble steps and vanished from view.

Zero grimaced. 'A great help, I must say. It's about time we got rid of all these doddering oldsters. I say they should be packed off to the Queensway Home for Old Mice.'

'If I may suggest,' suggested the Chosen mouse, 'this seems the perfect time for a head-count. Or perhaps someone would care to investigate that dark spooky corner?'

'On the tip of my tongue,' agreed Zero hastily. 'A head-count it is.' Not only a bully, but he was a coward too. Quickly he ordered the Mob into line, and motioned for the count to begin.

'One, two, three, four . . . .' Each mouse counted himself off. Soon the correct total of twenty-four was reached.

'Twenty-five, if you please,' again came that voice from the corner. The frightened Mob jumped into the air as one.

'We might as well face it,' said the Chosen mouse, languidly. 'The "one too many" is in that dark, spooky corner. Any volunteers?'

'I say the Sneak should go,' shouted the one-eyed Breaker mouse at the back. 'As a newly-promoted Scout, he could use the practice.'

Everyone thought this a good idea. The Sneak

thought it a lousy one, but he had little choice. Slowly, cautiously, he crept across the cellar floor. Soon his yellow stripe faded into the gloom. Seconds later he came scampering back. He looked vastly relieved. 'There's no one there,' he said breathlessly. 'And don't ask me to double-check, for my knees are buckling. I think it's an invisible ghost, or something.'

'Rubbish,' scoffed Zero. 'Did you search properly?'

'Every scary inch,' lied the Sneak First Class. He was suddenly indignant. 'I am a Scout after all. My best friend taught me the tricks of the trade.'

'I did not,' cried the fed-up sentenced mouse. 'Why, when you've ruined my life, must you speak so affectionately?'

'Determined to cook my goose, aren't you?' spat the Sneak. 'But you'll be disappointed. The spooky witness has vanished into thin air. But then witnesses are rarely reliable.'

He shouldn't have said that. There was a movement from the darkened corner. Presently a form emerged from beneath the roof-tile. Watched by the stunned and gaping Mob, Pentecost came trotting across the cellar floor. Soon he stood before Zero, his ears flopping over his eyes, the moonlight streaming in through the hole in the wall, bathing his humbly bowed head. The reaction of the Mob was disbelief. First they stared long and hard at Pentecost. Then their gaze centred upon the lounging Chosen mouse. Even he had stopped chewing, his eyes wide with surprise. For it was obvious at a glance that the two were as like as peas in a pod. From their brown and white pelts, to the tips of their drooping ears, they could have been identical twins. Zero, as shocked as anyone, at last found his voice. 'It's clear even to a fool,' he spluttered. 'In fact it's as clear as daylight. . . .'

'Moonlight,' corrected the Chosen mouse. He too had recovered his composure. 'Number twenty-five is standing in moonlight. It's still dark outside, you'll find.'

'It was a figure of speech,' shouted Zero. 'The point is, there is not . . . there never was . . . and there never will be a number twenty-five.'

'There I agree,' said the Chosen mouse. 'One can't just tag along on the tail of twenty-four, hoping for the best. If we allowed that there would be twenty-sixes lined up around the block. Where would it all end? By the way, have you noticed the uncanny likeness number twenty-five and I share? Just thought I'd mention it.'

'Twenty-five is an impostor,' yelled the desperate Sneak. 'He is trying to invent a vacancy for himself. He may even have his eye on my new Scouting post. Well it's filled. Let him fight his way up from the bottom as I have.'

'Is that true?' growled Zero, advancing upon a trembling Pentecost. 'Is that why you dashed round here and hid in the corner? In the hope of landing a job?'

'No,' whispered Pentecost. 'I arrived by accident. I was swept into your home without permission. It was while wondering what to do that I saw the terrible crime committed. I felt I had to speak out.'

'If you have evidence that can clear the Scout, it's too late,' warned Zero. 'If I were you, I'd start worrying about myself. Just half of your crimes would choke a bull. I intend to make up a list.'

'First things first, interrupted the Chosen mouse. 'Let the stranger speak, this could be entertaining. So tell us about this "terrible crime", small duplicate.'

'Well, I saw the striped one push something into the mouth of the accused,' stuttered Pentecost. 'I remember the Scout looked very surprised, as if he wasn't expecting it. And the striped mouse was rubbing his paws and smiling. Then when I heard the Scout sentenced for theft, I realised I had to do something.'

'So you decided to twit?' said the Sneak, venomously.

'We don't call it twitting on Lickey Top,' Pentecost raised a proud head. 'We call it fair play and justice.'

'But why should you, a stranger, risk your life for me?' asked the Scout. He was quite amazed.

'Because you are innocent,' was the reply.

'My, my, how very noble,' murmured the Chosen One. 'Fancy thinking of others at such a time . . . . Hello, our little saint has more to say.'

His mocking tone failed to put Pentecost off. He addressed the flummoxed Scout. 'I want you to know that I will stand by you no matter what.' Then to the Mob as a whole. 'I came to the city on the wings of destiny, and the ears of Fox of Furrowfield. It is my sacred mission to help overthrow a tyrant, and bring peace and happiness to the city. I do not need to steal one of your jobs, for I already have one back home. If I have committed a "crime" by defending the Scout, then I will commit many more in the future.' All this was delivered in ringing tones.

'Did you prepare that speech?' asked a suspicious Zero. 'It sounded very pat to me. We speak off the top of our heads in the city. Prepared speeches smack of the furrowed brow, and plenty of leisure. The Chosen mouse is a prime example of that, but we all have our crosses to bear. So enough of your haughty back-chat. Black Shadow will be enjoying two late suppers to-night. But first to list your crimes . . . for the record, you'll understand. . . .'

'Beware of mice too eager to condemn,' broke in the

56

Chosen mouse. He chewed thoughtfully. 'As I see it, the Scout has acquired fresh evidence to rest his case upon. Before we go any further let's see if their stories tally.'

'It's all going to come out,' yelled the wild-eyed Sneak. 'The Scout is about to break his "no twitting" rule. I am about to be dealt one of life's bitter blows.' He began to dash aimlessly about the cellar. The one-eyed Second Class Breaker promptly caught and sat upon him.

The Scout, however, remained true to his code. 'I will merely say I am innocent,' he said stubbornly. 'If you wish to believe the stranger's story, so be it. But I myself will stand or fall upon my own word. Nevertheless, I thank the uncanny double from the bottom of my soul. If that sounds grateful, I will exchange the remark for a curt nod in his direction.'

'I'm in with a chance yet,' whooped the Sneak. He had struggled free from his captor. 'The Scout has been thrown a life-line and what does he do? He refuses it. What kind of world is this where folk almost jostle to be Black Shadowed? I don't understand it, but I thoroughly approve.'

'Put this business to a vote,' said the Chosen mouse. He eyed Zero. 'That's if the Gas Street Mob still have that right?'

The Mob murmured their agreement. Unsure as always, Zero saw the writing on the wall. Personally, he had been looking forward to the double execution. He enjoyed spilling blood. But despite his backing bully-mice, he knew that to go against the wishes of the majority could spell only trouble. Like all tyrants, he lived in fear of popular revolution. Such a movement only needed a leader. This was why Zero watched the

Chosen mouse so carefully. And the honourable Scout. And the out-spoken one-eyed Breaker. In fact, Zero's suspicious eyes watched everyone, and now the stranger was added to his list. Cunningly, he trimmed his sails and became the reasonable leader. As usual he over-acted and fooled no one. 'I wouldn't say so before, but I have been on the side of the Scout all along,' he said, his watchful eyes daring anyone to scoff. 'In fact, my threats were but a test of the Mob's fairness. I am pleased to say you have all passed with flying colours. So I think we can dispense with the vote. The Scout First Class is granted a full pardon with my blessing.'

The Gas Street Mob nodded their approval. Zero then turned his evil gaze upon the cowering Sneak. 'As for you, I forthwith strip away your new Scouting post. You will return to decoying. And think yourself lucky to get off so lightly.'

'It's something, I suppose,' sighed the Sneak. 'And I have learned an important lesson. The secret of success is to be honest and popular. In the few days remaining to me, I aim to become the most honest and best-loved mouse in the Mob. We'll see how that goes.'

'Now to the next bit of business,' said Zero, relish in his voice. 'The Scout has got legally off the hook, but this interfering stranger certainly won't. The Mob will consider these facts. Forced entry into the cellar . . . claiming the number twenty-five, which doesn't exist . . . hiding in a corner with intent . . . emerging from a corner with intent . . . and lastly, impersonating the idle Chosen mouse. In short – '

'Someone is about to have the book thrown at him,' finished the Sneak gleefully. 'This constant desire to seek out victims for punishment is quite beyond me,' said the Chosen mouse, in a bored voice. 'It is the surest way to get oneself hated, if one isn't already. One's fall usually follows fast.'

Zero looked daggers. 'I suppose that crack is aimed at me?' His bitterness spilled over. 'In the old days a leader was respected and obeyed. Now it seems we bend over backwards to excuse the criminal. I suppose you are angling for a lenient vote again?'

Suddenly to everyone's surprise, the pardoned Scout took his stand at Pentecost's side. 'I wish to say a few words,' he said, clearing his throat. 'I'm not taking sides, mind. Just because this stranger cleared my name, it doesn't make him my chum. The truth is, I find close relationships embarrassing. However, I like to see justice done. This is why I stand here. Some of you may think my action warm-hearted. Others may feel I'm stand-offish. But one thing is clear. Here I stand and here I stay until we either hear this mouse out, or until Hell freezes over.'

The Mob, curious to learn more about the strange mouse in their midst, voiced their agreement, for city-mice enjoyed a good story. They settled down expectantly.

'Let him speak,' ordered Zero, though grudgingly. He glared at Pentecost. 'And remember, no rounded sentences, for I will soon twig a rehearsed speech.'

'Thank you,' said a much relieved Pentecost. 'I am grateful for this chance to clear myself. But first I must deny Zero's accusations. As a politely brought up mouse I am not in the habit of loitering with intent in the homes of other folk. And I have already said I am not in need of a precious job. I am Pentecost, chosen leader in my own land, sent by fate into the city to carry out the sacred mission I spoke of.'

There came a gasp from the Mob as they digested

59

these proud words. The lounging Chosen mouse had stopped chewing, his eyes intent upon the speaker. As for Zero, he was looking decidedly uneasy.

Pentecost continued. But now his voice was subdued, and tinged with sadness. 'But I was not a good leader, I realise that now. I became filled with envy. For it was always the old Pentecost they talked about. Every day my family would put fresh flowers on his grave to mourn his passing, and I, not wishing to understand, became more and more resentful. I believed I was being deliberately ignored. And then there was Fox who was everything I yearned to be, ever the hero, always jaunty and devil-may-care in his bright red coat. Fox, who I now realise was too kindly to mention the adventures he had shared with the old Pentecost for fear of hurting me. And what did I do? I repaid this kindness with harsh and bitter words. And then the Old Codger and Son arrived on Lickey Top from their round-the-world trip, having had to dodge the slings and arrows of life every step of the way. And when the Old Codger looked into my future and declared that I would go into the city to carry out a sacred mission, I foolishly jumped at the chance, even though I knew deep down it would be wrong to desert my family. But things went badly awry. Fox warned me not to accompany him here, but I would not listen. And he was right, for instead of doing heroic things, I found myself hiding like a coward in your cellar. It seems the Old Codger's gift has played a cruel trick on me, for doubtless Fox has washed his paws of me, and has returned home. And now I am alone, my mission in ruins. But whatever my fate, I can face it knowing that at least I did one unselfish thing in proving the innocence of the Scout First Class. My only regret is that my family will never know I faced death bravely. . . . ' Pentecost raised a weary head, and looked about him. 'I am now ready to meet my fate,' he ended quietly.

For a long time no-one spoke. The Scout, so stiff and friendless, wiped away a secret tear. In contrast Zero wore a broken-toothed sneer. He no longer felt uneasy. This broken mouse, this one-time leader before him, posed little threat to his own savage rule. But just in case, he made sure that the three bully-mice who hovered ever near him, were comfortingly close to hand. As for the rest of the Mob, the sad story had moved them. Noting this, the Sneak was racking his brains, trying to figure out just how the stranger mouse had managed to attract this sympathy. Was it some cunning secret he had not yet stumbled upon? A clever ploy to gain advancement? And what of the Chosen mouse? He was speaking now, his excitement mounting.

'Did you happen to journey here by way of Spaghetti Junction?' he asked quickly. 'And this "Fox" you speak of, could he be described as "a large red shape"?'

Pentecost considered this. 'Actually we travelled along Fox's private trail. And as for him being "a large red shape" – well, not by moonlight. But in the day-time he will often appear softly orange, sometimes a striking russet; but yes, indeed, red, the sun directly overhead. Why do you ask?'

'Because certain things are beginning to add up,' cried the Chosen mouse, jumping to his feet. 'Could this stranger be the lost and frightened mouse my old motor-way prophet spoke of? He says he was accidentally swept into our cellar. But was he? Perhaps fate meant him to be swept in here. But more interesting, didn't he say he journeyed to the city to carry out a sacred mission? And he mentions a place called Lickey Top. Now we know the city inside out. So how come we've never heard of this place? Isn't it a fact that most everywhere is within spitting distance of the Bull Ring shopping centre? I believe that this mouse is not a cunning job-stealer as Zero suggests, for there is more to him than meets the eye. I have a strange feeling that he and I have more in common than mere looks.'

'Where is all this nonsense leading?' snapped Zero. 'Who is interested in this piffle?'

'I am,' interrupted the impatient Chosen mouse. 'For I am beginning to believe that his Old Codger and my old motor-way prophet are one and the same. One more question will confirm it. Tell me, sweet reflection, can you recall a certain eccentric way of speaking . . . ?'

'Only that the Old Codger speaks through his son,' answered Pentecost, his own curiosity intense now. 'But that isn't so very odd, just practical. You see the Old Codger's jaws are constantly engaged in lunch. . . .'

'The pieces fit,' cried the triumphant Chosen one. He addressed the wide-eyed Mob. 'Now do you believe my incredible adventure on the Junction?' he shouted.

'Always,' yelled the awed Mob. 'Each and every sensible one of us.'

'Includes me also,' said the Sneak, hurriedly. 'For if my hunch is correct, the times they are a-changing. In short my loyalty is blowing in the wind, and I am ready to become a rolling stone.'

The excitement in the cellar was infectious. And with that excitement came stirring a long suppressed desire. Now there was a mood of revolution in the air. One could almost smell it. Although the Gas Street Mob had understood little of the exchange between Pentecost and the Chosen mouse, they were not slow to realise that something extraordinary was taking place. Could it be that the feared and hated Zero was about to be overthrown? Was there at this very moment a leader arising to lead them? A wild-eyed Zero was thinking much the same. Filled with a cowardly terror now, that fear made him doubly dangerous. Desperation came to his aid. Come Hell or high water he would do away with his potential rival, the Chosen mouse. The stranger, too, for was he not a leader in his own land, and thus an equal threat to Zero's rule? Ordering his menacing bullies close, he listened and watched, glowering with hate as the Mob voiced their pent-up feelings. And all the while he remained as tense as a coiled spring, awaiting his moment to act and destroy his enemies.

Now Zero and his bullies found themselves pressed against a wall, tight-ringed about by a hostile and scornful horde. The Chosen mouse, looking bewildered, had been shoved to the fore, many of the Mob eagerly glancing into his eyes as if waiting upon his word. Pentecost, also bewildered, and frightened, too, was lost amongst the jostling Mob. Then suddenly fickle fate intervened. Out of the corner of his eye Zero saw a shadow move to block out the moonlight streaming in through the hole from the dustbin alley outside. A dreadful howl, rising to a scream, froze the pushing and shoving Mob. Then swiftly a huge paw came thrusting into the cellar, needle-sharp claws threshing, searching . . . .

All thought of revolt and revenge was quickly forgotten. The petrified Mob began to trample each other underfoot in their haste to seek safety. Each corner of the cellar soon became crammed with pyramids of sobbing, heaving flesh as each mouse sought to save his own skin.

On a rotting rafter high above, a pair of coolly

observing eyes watched the frantic scramble below. Their owner was no stranger to the Gas Street cellar. In his search for new excitement and kicks, the watching cockle-snorkle had made it his business to pry into every nook and cranny of the city throughout his long life. It was his boast that not a blade of grass stirred anywhere in the Midlands without him knowing about it. Now the bug was congratulating himself that he had guessed right. That tiny, razor-sharp brain had long ago figured out that the action would be found in the Gas Street area. For wasn't this Fox's favourite foraging place? Now, gazing down, the gleeful insect could just make out the floppy-eared Pentecost mouse amidst that confused heap of bodies. Then he saw something that caused his heart to leap with delight. Intrigue indeed. Taking advantage of the furore Zero had seized and dragged from the pile a small, sad-eared mouse. Quickly the evil leader propelled him across the cellar to fling him headlong into those cruelly spiked claws. There was heard one despairing cry, the most pathetic of struggles, and then the paw withdrew, full. That was enough for the inquisitive cockle-snorkle. Zipping down from his perch, he buzzed the sobbing and uncaring Gas Street Mob as he sped out through the hole, and into the alley-way. He was just in time to see what happened there. . . .

All this time Fox had been holed up a street or two away, licking his wounds and trying to collect his bewildered thoughts. It had all happened so suddenly: the appearance of the impossibly huge and fierce Black Shadow, the desperate fight to save the Pentecost mouse, and his own terrified dash for safety. For a moment he had considered making straight for home, but now, having had time to think, he felt ashamed to even have considered it. For he knew, deep down, he could not desert his plucky friend. True, they had had their differences in the past, but a pal in need could always depend on the loyalty of Fox of Furrowfield. Rising painfully to his feet, Fox retraced his steps, hoping against hope that a miracle would occur, and that the dawn would find two friends homeward-bound. Arriving at Gas Street, he slipped behind a dustbin opposite the hole in the wall. He was not to know that a few bins down another waited. Green of eye, claws sprung for action, the great cat also watched that crumbling hole. . . .

Even as Black Shadow, impatient and frustrated now, launched himself forward, so a surprised Fox was on his feet. He heard the plaintive cry and the cat's triumphant mew, and prepared himself for action. When Fox saw that limp but familiar form clutched in that awful grip, he became a fighting fury. Soon he and Black Shadow were locked in combat once more. Over and over they rolled, crashing into dustbins, their life and death struggle sending lids bowling and crashing over the cobbles of the alley. Somehow during the fight the mouse was flung clear. With a thud his floppy-eared head hit the wall, leaving him slumped and unconscious as the battle surged around him. But Black Shadow was tiring. Soon he had had enough. Tearing free from Fox, he leapt for a bin-top, then for the wall, and was gone. . . .

The city receded to a crawl of bright light. Bloodied and shaken, Fox limped homewards. Soon the welcoming hills were looming higher and higher before his grateful eyes. But inside he still seethed with anger. The urge to vent his feelings was strong in him, but he held his peace, wearied paws ever eating away the miles. Soon he was climbing into the foothills, his breathing

65

laboured, wounds stiffening as the bleeding stopped and dried. Only once did he pause to rest. Thankfully he sucked great gulps of air into his lungs. Then he was up and off again, the unconscious mouse nipped firmly between gentled teeth, swinging in the first light of dawn. . . .

'Little bug, you've had a busy day . . . and night,' grinned the cockle-snorkle. 'And now you too get yourself home, for there is where the action will be.' From drab to lemon, to bright orange, he prepared himself for flight. Soon he was winging high over the city towards the lightening Lickey Hills.

4 *A Most Unseemly Mouse*

Owl's nerves had been at snapping point all night. He had barely managed to snatch a wink of sleep. He had passed away those dark hours with his foot hanging outside his home. His hope had been that the cool autumn breezes might ease the dreadful throbbing. They had not. Owl now believed he was a victim of frost-bite, for the pre-dawn hours had been nippy. And if that wasn't enough, he had been forced to endure throughout the sound of the hedgehogs, grinding their supper at the foot of his tree. And there was more. Just after dawn, as the bird had managed to doze off, the bug had returned from somewhere or other. The insect had perched on the edge of his hole, bubbling with excitement as he told his master the latest news. But Owl had his own problems, and couldn't have cared less. Angrily he snapped at the bug, telling him to leave him in peace and go bother someone else. As the sun rose red and cheerless, so the sleepless bird cursed roundly and soundly. Taking the hint, the bug fleww off down the hill. As he had expected, Uncle had told his family the news. They were kicking up a terrible fuss. Truly maddened now, Owl poked his head outside and yelled for some peace and quiet.

'I am attempting to keep everything low-key,' shouted back Uncle. 'I suppose you've heard the sad news, Owl? I have known all night. I couldn't sleep with the worrying.'

'That makes two of us,' retorted the bird. 'So go worry somewhere else. Why so close to my tree, for pity's sake?'

'Because it's shady,' shouted the young mice. 'Uncle Pentecost tends to suffer blinding headaches in the direct sunshine.'

For a brief moment Owl's eyes widened in surprise. But they soon drooped sleepily again. He drifted off into an uneasy slumber.

'I don't think my master is too impressed by Uncle's self-promotion,' commented the bug, flying down to join the circle of anxious mice.

'And I am not impressed by Owl's attitude,' retorted the old mouse. 'I detected a threatening tone. Surely he must realise I am trying frantically to cope with my sudden fame? A little pity from that selfish bird would not go amiss.'

'Everything is a pity in my opinion,' remarked a worried great aunt. She and her sisters continued to weave grass-stems, but because of the distressing news about Pentecost the patterns they wove were without shape.

'Nevertheless, a move down the hill would be kind,' remarked another. 'Thus leaving Owl and his problems in the Land of Nod.' And this the family did.

The circle they formed was a large one. Even the morning food-gatherers were there, for who felt like breakfast at such a time? In the centre sat Uncle, trying to appear confident and stern at the same time. He wasn't finding it easy. But then he had little flair for anything. Swaying on a grass-stalk close beside him was the especially cheerful bug. The chattering family fell silent as both Uncle and the insect cleared their throats.

'After you,' said the gracious bug. 'For what I have to say will take longer. You have only heard the bare bones of my story.'

'Thank you.' Uncle addressed the gathering, his voice grave. 'This is an emergency. That is why I have been forced out of retirement. I have been implored by many mice to grasp the empty reins of leadership. The plain facts are, we have been deserted by the Pentecost mouse. At this moment he is doing his own thing in the city. During the night while you were peacefully sleeping, I was listening with red eyes to the story of the cockle-snorkle . . . .'

'But only a sketchy outline of the same,' said the bug quickly. 'I didn't go into details. I am saving those for this meeting.'

'So without more ado I hand you over to the rare cockle-snorkle,' said Uncle grandly.

'The rise of Uncle is no longer a nightmare,' cried Old Mother, rocking back and forth in anguish. 'Now I am dreading to hear the bug's details, for certain gnarled paws and thoughts will surely take advantage of them.'

'Quiet, please!' shouted Uncle. Then with a respectful glance up the hill at the browsing hedgehogs, 'Lunch

68

manners excepted, of course. Carry on, Cockle-snorkle.'

'Well, you can all dry your eyes for a start,' announced the insect. 'It's true Fox and the Pentecost mouse went to the city. But at this point I must contradict Uncle. You see, old cunning-chops and a certain mouse are no longer there. They are even now on their way home, and a sorrier pair I've yet to see. So let's have a few smiles shining through those tears, eh? We'll have another good cry later. In fact, quite soon, I'm thinking.'

The significance of those last remarks was lost on the now gladdened harvest mice. Uncle, taken by surprise by the bug's statement, was at a loss. He hadn't expected his reign to be quite so short. But he was secretly relieved by the news. However, he remained stern as he spoke again.

'So, they returned from the jaws of danger?' he said, grimly. 'No doubt they will soon be boasting about their exploits in the city? But will they spare a thought for the worry they have caused? I think not. Well, I for one will have a few sharp words with that scally-wag Pentecost.'

'Whatever have you been playing at?' said Old Mother gently. 'That is the question I will put to our leader. But thank the Lord he is returning, scally-wagged it's true, but safe and sound, that's the main thing. And when we do greet him, we will promise never to ignore him again. I have long noticed him sitting alone upon the hill, looking in puddles for company.'

'I didn't say anything about "safe and sound",' the bug pointed out. 'I have been holding something back. My teasing nature, you'll understand.'

'Remember the words of my dad,' warned the Son. The hedgehogs, now glutted with snails, had decided to take a breather. They joined the circle. 'Remember, the mouse will not be what he seems. . . .'

Before any of the curious mice could ask the meaning of these strange words, a sharp-eyed mouse jumped to his feet, shouted and pointed down the hill. All the family stood to crane. Soon everyone could make out the familiar figure, toiling up the hill.

'There will be no kindly words spoken,' said Uncle, sharply. 'Let them scan our faces and see only blank contempt.'

'If Fox tries to cuff and roll us, we will stalk away with high noses,' vowed the little ones. They ran to hide behind the two green hillocks which were the Old Codger and Son. But any unkind thoughts the harvest mice

might have harboured soon turned to pity. They could all see the state Fox was in. To hear the harsh rasp of his breathing, to view the dried blood clinging to his fur, was to realise that the red creature was in no mood for argument, let alone play. Halting outside the circle, he dropped his limp burden into the grass. 'I think this belongs to you?' His eyes were dull, his voice heavy with fatigue. He turned to depart, throwing a final remark over an aching shoulder. 'And when he comes round, tell him from me that I told him so. Tell him I warned him of what might happen in the city. I only hope he's learned his lesson.' Soon his wearied form was trudging back down the hill. He vanished into the Weasel Woods. The circle quickly broke as the family crowded around the crumpled but recognisable body of their leader. As they stared, awaiting signs of life, many began to fidget uneasily. It was Uncle who voiced the dreaded words. 'I think he has passed quietly away.' His tone was subdued. 'Furrowfield limped home alone through the trails and pastures. He couldn't have known that he was cursing a dead friend from the side of his clenched jaw. If it's any comfort at all, the family can call me Uncle Pentecost once more.'

But as usual, the old mouse was jumping the gun. The eyes of the 'dead' leader were beginning to flutter open. A paw twitched, a floppy ear turned inside-out. A tail, complete with sore-looking teeth-marks, flicked feebly. Soon the mouse was sitting up and looking about him in astonishment. Immediately, two sturdy mice leapt forward to assist as he staggered to his feet. They then began to lead him around in small circles to help clear his head. After a while he was able to stand unaided. With cries of relief, the family crowded around him.

'Stand back,' ordered Uncle. 'Our leader needs to gulp lots of fresh, hilly air.' The mice drew back.

It was then 'Pentecost' began to act very strangely indeed. Watched by the puzzled mice, he stopped to pick from the ground a crackling red leaf. There was wonder in his eyes as he crushed it into a thousand fragments, allowing them to be whirled away by the breeze into a blue sky. His enchantment was moving to see, and the family, not wishing to intrude upon this private joy, held their peace. Surely his actions were those of a repentant mouse, simply happy to be home? Warmed by his mood, the mice silently forgave him his follies. It was only when he began to speak that the watchers felt anger once more. For instead of apologising for the worry he had caused, he took not the slightest notice of them. Instead, he seemed to be dreaming aloud. But what made it so shocking was that his musings were voiced in the crudest of accents. 'Why does he ramble of prophets and destinies?' whispered Old Mother. 'And not in his lilting country speech, but with vowels like those of a corn-crake?'

'Pentecost is getting above himself with such talk,' snorted an aunt.

'Whatever have you been playing at?' chided Old Mother. 'It's a question that must be asked.'

The mouse ignored her. He was frowning. 'Why is my tail smarting so?' he asked himself, tenderly inspecting it.

Uncle marched up to him. 'We are still not satisfied with what you haven't said,' he rapped furiously. 'You run off with the leadership, and expect it to be here when you return? I hope you realise the severity of my words?' He continued to badger the lounging mouse, for now lounging he was, a pink nose turned to the sun as if to brown it.

'You will be the local comic,' said the mouse, sitting up. 'Or are you just cracked in the head? Can't a Chosen mouse enjoy his destiny in peace? Go pester someone else.'

'Cracked he may be,' said the indignant little ones. 'But he is your caring uncle for all that.'

'Now he's my uncle,' grimaced the mouse. 'That's all I need.'

'Of course I'm your treasured uncle,' yelled Uncle. 'When are you going to thank me for keeping the family closely-knit in your absence? But for my firmness, they would have fled away in small nervous units. When are you going to dish out some blame to yourself? As Pentecost and leader, you should be ashamed to face your family.'

'Let's get this straight.' The mouse was beginning to look worried and perplexed. 'How I got here I don't know, but I am, and there's an end to it. But an uncle I don't know from Adam, I don't need. Next, so help me, you are going to say that this rabble is the bunch of mice my old prophet expects me to lead? Well, if that's the case, frankly I wish I'd stayed in the city. A beautiful place this might be, but you lot are becoming a pain in the neck. Complain and nag is all you've done since I arrived.'

'Pentecost has rejected us,' said Uncle, bitterly. 'A few hours in the city, and he returns with chosen airs and graces. We have become trash in his eyes. Furrowfield made a grave mistake in bringing him home.'

'Who's he when he's at home?' queried the other. 'Not another cracked uncle, I couldn't bear that.'

'He has even forgotten his close friend Fox,' remarked a saddened Old Mother. 'If only the city had been put out of bounds. It has turned our Pentecost's head with its slick, fast pace.'

'Fox, you say?' the mouse was all interest. 'Large, red and shapely? Am I getting warm?'

'He foolishly carried you home,' said Uncle, shaking his grey old head. 'But at least your memory is coming back. Soon you will beg our forgiveness, and crave another chance. But I warn you, we are thinking of slinging you out on your ugly ear, and second chances

73

come only three or four times in a mouse's lifetime. You will now explain yourself.'

'Well,' began the mouse, settling comfortably. 'It all started a week ago when I got lost on Spaghetti Junction. Anyway, I was just about to give my neck, when out of the choking fumes crawled an old prophet and son. . . . ' And on he went, spinning a tale so incredible that the family crowded around so as not to miss the end bit. The exception was Old Mother. Her face was creased with concern as she sat alone, gazing at the hedgehogs browsing round the edge of the circle. The strange words of the Old Codger were ringing in her ears. 'The mouse . . . he is not what he seems,' murmured the Son, as if reading her mind.

The teller had finished his story and was now gazing in amazement at the pair. 'Well, knock me down with a number nine bus!' he shouted. 'If it isn't my old motorway prophet and son. What are you doing up here? I was imagining you squashed flat as pancakes on the Junction. Well, you were right about the beautiful place. But I have got one complaint. It's this rabble here. They're wearing me ragged. They keep calling me Pentecost for some reason. And you see that old mouse there . . . he reckons he's my uncle. I deny it, of course. Who in their right mind would take him on as a close relative? But most worrying of all, this bunch seem to think I'm their leader. Please, by all that's holy, put me out of my misery and say I'm not. Frankly, if this set-up is what my destiny has in mind, I'd rather forget the whole thing.'

'My dad's gift warned there would be confusion,' replied the Son. 'You are here for a purpose. Live and learn, and in the meantime enjoy your lunch. All will be revealed when the time is ripe; so speaks my dad who is feeling giddy, and doubts if he will last until mid-day. Please don't tire him any more.' With that the Son buried his nose into the nettles for a quick snack.

'If only the family would cotton on,' beseeched Old Mother, her eyes moistening again.

'Cotton on to what?' asked Uncle, dumbly. 'And why does the Pentecost mouse suddenly fear for his sanity? I too am beginning to feel giddy with it all.'

At long last the cockle-snorkle broke his silence. The family, with so much on their minds, had forgotten about him. Being so distressed, they had not noticed the violently swaying grass-stalk. All this time the insect had fought to contain his impatient glee. He could control himself no longer. A spare leg, quivering with excitement, pointed first at the returned mouse, and then at the confused family. Words poured forth in a torrent.

'Fools, idiots!' he screamed. 'You've been tricked. That is not the Pentecost mouse. A simpleton with half an ear would have twigged it long ago. Must I spell it out for you? That mouse is a cunning double who has wormed his way on to Lickey Top, while your real leader suffers agonies in the city. It so happens I spent the better part of last night there, watching the goings-on. And I'll tell you something else. I know who is at the bottom of all this. I name that culprit Fox of Furrowfield, your leader's so-called best friend. What do you think about that?' he ended, triumphantly.

'Steady on,' protested the Chosen mouse. '"Worming my way up here", that's a bit strong?'

'I knew it!' cried Uncle, stomping angrily up and down. 'The moment I set eyes on that mouse! And didn't the Old Codger say he would not be what he seemed . . . ?'

'Nonsense,' snapped an aunt. 'You were taken in like the rest of us. Sit down, you old good-for-nothing. Now is the time to mourn, not crow.'

The bug interrupted. He had more to say. 'There is worse to come, I'm afraid. Control your tempers, for I have to inform you it was Fox who persuaded Pentecost to go to the city. And when that unwilling mouse arrived he was immediately seized and carried off by a rascally band of mice calling themselves the Gas Street Mob. The family, by the way, of that Chosen mouse there. Fox, of course, ran for his life. But later he met up with this double, and they made a deal. That impostor, well known in the city as a washed-out layabout, agreed to impersonate Pentecost, for he fancied a soft, easy life on Lickey Top. All this fitted nicely into Fox's plans, for he was too cowardly to rescue the genuine article. He chose the scoundrel's way out. He believed if he carried home something similar, no-one would be the wiser. That's where he made his mistake, for anyone can see this mouse is not the real Pentecost.'

'My dad says all the lies in the world will not alter the path of destiny,' broke in the Son. 'A mouse was fated to go to the city. A mouse was fated to return. There is a lot more fate in the pipe-line, but my dad is too weak to discuss it at the moment.'

'Fate and destiny is all very well, but it must not be allowed to upset our orderly lives,' said a sensible aunt. 'A solution to our problems must be found, and quickly. Pentecost must be rescued, and that smelly stand-in returned to whence he came.'

'I'll have you know this is none of my doing,' protested the Chosen mouse. 'I've never laid eyes on this Fox, so how could we make a deal? All I remember is being thrown to Black Shadow, the rest is a blank.'

'A likely story,' scoffed Uncle. 'You and Furrowfield are partners in crime, don't deny it. As the Old Codger said, you would return and be the cause of great . . . it must be hate.' The family were by now convinced of this. Many wept. Others stared in stony anger at the Chosen mouse. The cockle-snorkle had done a good job. He was particularly pleased that Fox's good name was now mud. 'As leader I will tax my brain for the next step,' announced Uncle, importantly. 'I shall stroll thoughtfully along the bank of Wending Way stream for a few days, until a solution leaps instantly to mind. . . .'

'Don't bother,' said the bug. 'I already have a remedy. It is a carefully staged plan. First a deputation, second a confrontation, third an explanation, fourth and last, an ending to this situation.'

'If the rescue attempt proves as difficult as the words of the plan, I see no hope for our Pentecost,' grieved Old Mother. 'Perhaps something simpler . . . ?'

'Very well,' the bug replied. 'We will simply march down to the Lowlands, and demand that Fox sort this mix-up out. In short, we have suffered a switch, but now know who's which. So when shall we set off? Time isn't on our side, remember. The city mice might grow tired of torturing the Pentecost mouse, and bump him off.'

'The bug is right,' said Uncle, briskly. 'I, of course, will lead this deputation. It is well known that I have a disturbing effect on Furrowfield. I need only stand before him, clenching and unclenching my paws, and he will become a broken reed. So if the phoney Pentecost is ready to travel . . . or must I put these feared paws to good use . . . ?'

'Oh good, I could do with stretching my legs,' said

the cheeky Chosen mouse, climbing to his feet. 'And perhaps you would point out the spots of special beauty along the way. You know, the stuff that dreams are made of . . . quiet dells and shady nooks, thrush-packed bushes, and tinkling brooks . . . ?'

'I'll do better than that,' growled Uncle. 'One false move from you, and the brook will be tinkling over your head. You can keep the date with your partner Furrowfield or one with a peckish perch. I don't care which. . . .'

And so the angry deputation set off down the hill. In the lead was Uncle, then came two tough mice, in case of trouble, then a gaggle of little ones who refused to go back and the bug winging overhead. Dawdling behind and ignoring Uncle's angry shouts came the Chosen mouse. Often he paused to sniff, his city-bred nose glorying in the country air, an invisible but heady wine to such as he. Ambling along, his thoughts ranged back and forth. He had come to terms with the strange things that had happened so far. He was under no illusions. He guessed that his future held more of the same. But he was confident that, while in the hands of fate, he would be protected. Hardened by a life-time in the city, he was not much bothered that the Lickey Top mice chose to treat him like a leper. He had experienced much the same back home. Besides, after listening to the argument that had raged about him only recently, he could understand the hostility of the country mice. For a while he had been mystified as to the identity of this 'Pente-cost' mouse. But now he knew. He was remembering the stranger who bore such a remarkable resemblance to himself, trotting from the cellar corner to clear the Scout's good name. He could only be the 'lost and frightened soul-mate' the old prophet had told him

would suffer until he himself returned to put things right. Well, he certainly wasn't going to worry about that unfortunate mouse right now. He would let things take their course. In the meantime he would make the most of his break from the mean city. Didn't the sun feel warm upon his bedraggled and grubby fur? And what a relief that he could, for a while, drop his guard. For here there was no Zero to protect himself against. No in-fighting for survival, as back in the Gas Street cellar. For where was the enemy here? Certainly not amongst this bunch of countrified innocents. So they despised him? But wasn't it better to be despised in this heaven, then to be constantly guarding his back in the Hell he had left behind? Fate led him through the peace of the Lickey Hills, holding him close, for he was a Chosen one. . . .

5 Decoy Third Class

It was mid-day in the Gas Street Cellar. The whole of the Mob was congregated, for there was a small remem-

79

brance service taking place. The speakers, evil and corrupt, were putting on quite a show. Zero and the Sneak were discussing the death of the Chosen mouse in pious tones. Zero hoped that by appearing humble and sad the suspicions of the family would be lulled. The Sneak had his reasons, too. At long last the leader had recognised his existence. Hadn't he promoted him to Scout First Class, if only for a minute or two? But it had been long enough. For a few brief moments the Sneak had experienced life at the top, and he had adored every fleeting second. True, he had been brought down with a bump, but the delicious memory lingered. He intended to visit those heady heights again, but next time to stay there. His plan was all worked out. He meant to stick so close to Zero that the other would come to regard him as a second skin. He would become a 'nodding mouse', agreeing with every word his leader said. He would so butter Zero up . . . of course, at the same time the Sneak would be keeping his eyes open, and his ear to the ground. At the slightest hint that Zero's rule was about to crumble, the Sneak would drop him like a hot brick, and become the nodding mouse of another. But for the moment Zero had regained control again. The threatened revolt had been timely nipped in the bud by the appearance of Black Shadow. Now the Mob felt too dispirited to continue their action. They could only listen in miserable silence as the lies passed back and forth between Zero and his new-found friend. To back them up, the three bully-mice stood eyeing the subdued group, and punching their paws in a menacing way.

'He was a trier,' Zero was saying, shaking his head in sorrow. 'Always remember, to try yet fail is not the end of the world. One just keeps trying and trying until success is achieved. For, my friends, if the Chosen mouse was anything, he was a good trier.' The bully-mice mumbled their agreement. There were many watering mouths and rumbling stomachs in the cellar, as that trio chewed away at their extra cheese-ration. Zero addressed the Mob: 'And now, a moment's silence for a lost brother.' He bowed his head; the mice, Pentecost amongst them, following his example.

'That's enough,' said Zero, briskly. 'You can mourn a little more in your own time. I certainly will. But now, back to the problem we were discussing before Black Shadow interrupted us. I'm talking about the stranger in our midst. Are we all agreed he is some kind of spy, from a rival Mob, perhaps? Are we of a mind that he is a danger to us, and should be done away with?'

'No,' said the pardoned Scout, firmly. 'I for one believe his story. I am sure his presence here is accidental. He says he comes from a distant place to help overthrow a tyrant, and bring peace and happiness to the city. Surely that is no crime?'

'All depends who the tyrant is,' muttered the Sneak. 'Ask him who he has in mind.'

Hearing this, Pentecost stepped forward. 'I don't know,' he said, miserably. 'The Old Codger was a little vague on that point.'

'Well, the mouse has my respect and admiration,' continued the Scout, in ringing tones. 'Not my friendship, you understand, for I always shy away from close bonds. But I feel that such a much-travelled mouse will have picked up skills that could prove useful to the Mob. I think a post should be found for him. I say this not because he saved my life, but because his talents can only benefit us.'

'I second that,' said the one-eyed Breaker. 'And if a

certain leader doesn't want another out-break of trouble, he will agree, too.'

Fuming inside, Zero nevertheless fell in with their wishes. Just as well, for most of the Mob were siding with the two brave mice. It was the Sneak, ever desperate for promotion, who came up with the idea that brought a guarded and evil smile to the leader's face.

'He can have my job,' urged the Sneak. 'I won't mind in the least.'

'That seems fair,' replied Zero, stroking his whiskers and trying to appear wise. 'For we all must start at the bottom.'

'And what is lower than a Decoy Third Class?' went on the jubilant Sneak. 'Take my word for it, it's the pits. Of course, I will have to rise to make room for him.'

'Very well, he will train under you. Consider yourself a newly-graded Decoy Second Class,' said Zero, giving him a pat. He glared at Pentecost. 'Do you accept our generous offer?'

'I do,' came the faint reply.

'And may God have mercy on your soul,' said the happy Sneak. 'At last I'm top-dog over somebody. At last I can do some ordering about, and pile all the risk on to someone else. I can see the new Decoy and me becoming very close friends. Would he like that?'

'Very much,' shuddered Pentecost. 'Thank you very much.'

'That's settled then,' said Zero. 'Welcome to the Gas Street Mob, Decoy Third Class.'

'I'm much obliged,' replied the leader of Lickey Top, humbly. 'I promise to do my very best.'

'You will be sworn in after lunch,' said Zero. Then, warningly, 'The oath, of course, being binding unto death. You realise that?'

Pentecost nodded apprehensively. 'So let's go in,' said the impatient one-eyed mouse. 'I don't know about you lot, but I'm famished.' It seemed everyone was. Without more ado, Zero leading the way, the Mob filed through the alcove into the parlour.

Ordinarily, city-mice have little time for polite manners. But there is one exception to this rule. The acquiring of food is a dangerous pursuit, and, it being so scarce, makes for ritual. Meal-times in the Gas Street cellar were always special occasions. All personal squabbles were, during such times, forbidden by law. Rank was set aside, thus making every mouse equal. In this relaxed gathering, skills and wisdoms were passed on to the young. In this way the Mob survived and thrived, and the breaking of tomorrow's cheese was assured. Pentecost was quickly found a place next to the Scout. Much to his distaste, the Sneak shoved in to seat himself on the other side. But the country mouse could hardly protest. He knew he was lucky to be alive at all. Suddenly, Zero signalled, and silence fell over the hungry mice. The old mouse who counted folk in and out rose to say a small prayer.

'For what we have pinched from the city,
May the Lord make us truly thankful. . . .'

Afterwards it was time to relax. The latest news was gossipped about, the sad death of the Chosen mouse being a popular topic. A bachelor and a misfit, nevertheless his end was discussed with respect. But it was the presence of Pentecost that excited most comment. His startling likeness to the late Chosen mouse was much bandied about. And then Zero was rising, motioning for silence again.

83

'As most of you will know, we have taken on a new Decoy,' he began. Then churlishly, 'Let us hope he works as hard as he scoffs. He must have shovelled down the rations of three mice, at least.'

'I gave him a portion of mine,' explained the Scout. 'Not because I wish a friendship to blossom, but because he must be very hungry after his journeying. The gesture of giving and receiving naturally passed without a smile. We remain as always, poles apart.'

'We are not here to discuss your personal hang-ups,' snapped Zero. Then his snout twisted into what he imagined to be a smile. 'During lunch some of you may have noticed a tear dripping off my whiskers? You might have thought, "poor Zero, with all his heavy responsibilities to bear"? How many of you, I wonder, are now regretting your hasty and hurtful accusations made against me? But I have never borne a grudge. To prove it I have decided to revive an ancient Gas Street custom. I refer to the old after-lunch Question Time. For the young who cannot remember, this was a hard-hitting and free discussion when the leader was humbly obliged to answer for his actions. I am aware many of you are burning with anger that I should agree to take this stranger mouse into our midst. "He could be a dangerous spy," many of you may be whispering. "We must get Zero to reverse his kind decision," some of you may be quietly thinking. Well, even a leader must be ruled by the majority. So let Question Time commence.'

'I have a question,' piped up a small mouse. He sat snuggled up close to the Sneak. In fact they were father and son. He voiced his complaint. 'Why has my dad not been promoted higher? As a growing mouse I need the security of a father in a high position. I . . . I – '

'I cry for hours when . . .' hissed the Sneak, from the side of his mouth.

'I cry for hours when he is late home from a cheese-raid,' sobbed the youngster. 'I would shout for joy if he were raised to Scout First Class.'

'He was,' replied Zero brusquely. 'But he was broken to the ranks again.'

'I expect he was accused of framing someone?' was the bitter response. The small mouse seemed to know his father very well.

'Couldn't we drop the subject?' butted in the Scout. 'I find it deeply distressing.'

'I agree,' said Zero. Hopefully, he scanned the faces of the Mob. 'So who wishes to chastise me for unfairly employing this stranger mouse when my motto should be Mob first?'

The Scout, the one-eyed mouse, and many others quickly realised Zero's game. He was hoping to swing the Mob over to his side. His determination to get rid of Pentecost was becoming an obsession. What was it about that apparently harmless mouse that aroused such hatred? And fear, many began to realise. Surely Zero didn't see him as a rival? But then he must, for why was he so anxious to get rid of him? Could it be Zero believed himself to be that tyrant the small mouse was meant to help overthrow? But no matter. The decision to employ him had been made, and honour demanded that there could be no going back on it.

Unwittingly, it was the old mouse who counted folk in and out, who prevented yet another clash. Not only did this skill make him feel useful, but he also fervently believed that such devotion was the reason why he hadn't been banished to the Queensway Home for Old Mice. For some time he had sat burning with indignation. A stickler for correct table-manners, he loudly voiced his complaint. 'I would like to know why the new mouse has not the grace to thank us for the meal he has shared. Does he not realise how hard-won his lunch was?'

'I thank you all from the bottom of my heart,' said Pentecost sincerely. 'I would have thanked you before, but I was so very hungry. I would like to say it was a nice lunch.'

'Nice?' the old mouse wheezed. He lurched to his feet, looking deeply offended. Other mice seemed equally shocked. Pentecost realised he had committed some gaff, but couldn't for the life of him think what. He twisted uncomfortably as the old one quickly put him in the picture.

'Stale bread-crumbs are nice,' he shouted. 'And chocolate-cake is extremely nice. But best cheddar for lunch is something else entirely. It is the food of the Gods. It is highly splendid. It makes one smile a lot. Surely you felt the urge to smile when you first tasted it?'

'I did,' replied Pentecost, trying to repair the damage. 'In fact, I giggled out loud once. Being used to sweet-roots and a little wheat from time to time, I wasn't prepared to be amused. We don't have best cheddar on Lickey Top, more's the pity.'

'Lickle Tip,' corrected Zero, still fuming that his cunning plan to oust Pentecost had failed. He went on, attempting to impress with his knowledge. 'I know the place well. It is a mere spitting distance from the Bull Ring. I have strolled past many times and never noticed it.'

'It sounds slick and foreign to me,' said his old father. 'No wonder this new mouse fled the place. I put it down to the flooding of the city with these fast-paced modern cheeses, all tasteless, and full of holes. . . .'

'Shut your mouth, old mouse,' said Zero, abruptly. 'Take care you don't find yourself fast-paced to the Queensway Home. The arrangements can easily be made. This Question Time isn't for the likes of you. It is Mob business.' The old mouse gulped fearfully, but nobly recovered control. The square of his shoulders and snout were evidence of this. It was no accident that during his own time of leadership he had been known as Zero the Stubborn. He was proud of the fact that he had always stubbornly defended the rights of the old and the under-mouse. Such good days, the Mob often agreed wistfully.

'Let us not argue amongst ourselves,' pleaded the Scout. 'For myself I would like to listen to the sad events that drove the new Decoy into our cellar. And while he is speaking I will not point out that he is sitting much to close to me. I will not mention the fact that I prefer to keep the nicest of mice at paw-length. To blurt out these things would be to fall prey to one's emotions. I will simply point out that I am unable to point out such embarrassments.' A confused Pentecost took the hint, and sidled away. The Scout visibly relaxed.

'Lickle Tip,' pondered the one-eyed mouse. 'Is your old home as bad as it sounds?'

'Worse,' lied Pentecost. He still felt very nervous in the company of these tough, unpredictable mice. His sole ambition was under no circumstances to annoy them. He began to describe Lickey Top to the attentive gathering in an honest but unattractive way.

'Well, really it's an ordinary hill-top, with silly buttercups growing on it. On fine days we sit for hours, gazing at the boring blue hills of Clent. Sometimes we stroll down to the soaking-wet tinkling stream over Wending Way, and dangle our hot paws in the water. At night we have to put up with the whistling of many drab nightingales, and watch the rain-clouds drift over the ghostly moon. It isn't a very nice place, I'm afraid.'

'If this Lickle Tip is anywhere near the Bull Ring, I'm a Dutch-uncle,' declared the old mouse. His tone was adamant. 'I too know the city like the back of my paw, and I say no such place exists. Birds never whistle, they all sit upon the wires, nursing bad coughs. Zero says this place is near the Bull Ring . . . I say it cannot be.'

'I don't know where he finds the courage,' cried the bewildered Sneak. 'He knows he's just an old dodderer, getting under our paws. Yet still he finds the nerve to call our leader a liar. Surely he can't believe blood is thicker than water? For myself, everything Zero says is Gospel. I will take the liberty of awarding myself two merit marks for that.'

Still the old mouse wasn't finished. But despite his spirited stand, he was a pitiful sight. His eyes were white-filmed and peering. He had at some time lost most of his tail, a mere stump remaining. His yellowed teeth wobbled in their sockets as he spoke. At that moment Pentecost's heart went out to him. The old mouse reminded him so much of Uncle, back home. But then he realised there was little inner similarity. For here stood a life-scarred mouse, with true cause to be bitter. After a lifetime of good work, what had he to look forward to, but the Home for Old Mice? It was like being thrown on the scrap-heap. Looking at him, Pentecost could imagine how hardship and hunger had moulded his attitudes. He had obviously seen many terrible things, and his cynical out-look was proof that he had not liked what he saw. Now his eyes were seeking out the young mice in the circle.

'I will take advantage of this free-speaking period to put forward the case of the old, and so-called useless Mob members . . . ' he began, bravely.

'The free question and answer time is over,' shouted Zero irately. 'The next business is the swearing-in of the new Decoy.'

'I will be heard,' shot back the old mouse, his voice firm. Ignoring his son's angry protests, he addressed the giggling youngsters. 'You may think me an old fool, but let me tell you I was once filled with vigour, and a zest for life like you. The city was an exciting place then, for I could slip and slide with the best. I too yearned to be a fully-fledged Mob member, and experience the excitements and dangers of a cheese-raid.' He then spoke to Pentecost solely, his tone scornful. 'So you have come from a beautiful place within your head, to change our real world? You say you have a mission to help overthrow a tyrant, and bring peace and happiness to the city? So why do you tremble? Why do you humbly request to join the Mob as a suicidal Decoy Third Class? Are those the actions of a hero? You are beginning to realise there are no heroes in the city, only survivors. Well it's too late for regrets, for what the city attracts it keeps and finally destroys. Dwell on my words, stranger mouse.'

Pentecost had never felt so alone before. And he was indeed trembling. In truth, ever since he had entered the cellar, fear had been his only companion. Where was the mouse who had set out on his mission so confidently? He was here, trapped and bewildered, and at the mercy of a circle of hard-bitten and staring mice. Beside him, the Sneak seemed to sense his misery.

'Feeling down, are we?' he whispered. 'Never mind, I'll

look after you. After all, what are best friends for? Take no notice of the old one. He is sour because he's gone down in the world. The way to happiness is up, and we, true friends, will rise together.' He draped a skinny paw about the sobered mouse. Pentecost longed to shrug off that loathsome grip, but feared to. He was aware now the Sneak intended to use him to prolong his own life. Escape was Pentecost's only hope. But how? Desperately he tried to re-trace in his mind the route he and Fox had entered the city by. But he could not think clearly. In those few seconds all hope ebbed away. But no, one tiny spark remained. He vowed there and then that if he must die, he would do so bravely. And as he so resolved it seemed as if the spirit of the old Pentecost appeared before him, to offer comfort.

'Take heart and fight,' an inner voice urged. 'For though you feel it, you are not alone.' Then a harsh voice broke into that quiet moment. He was back in the reality of the cellar again, looking up into the coldly staring eyes of Zero.

'Are you ready to take the oath?' he asked, his voice deadly soft. He turned to walk into the centre of the circle, motioning Pentecost to follow. Shakily, the country mouse obediently rose. Soon they stood eye to eye, the Mob hushed and tensely watching.

'You will repeat after me: I solemnly swear in the presence of the Gas Street Mob . . .'

'I solemnly swear in the presence of the Gas Street Mob,' whispered Pentecost.

' . . . that as long as I live I will remain loyal and true. . . .' Stumbling, Pentecost repeated the words.

' . . . and will do my duty as a Decoy Third Class to the best of my ability,' rapped Zero.

' . . . to the best of my ability,' finished Pentecost.

'. . . and will until my dying day be faithful to that vow, which if I break, will mean my being hunted down, and put to death.'

'. . . will mean my being hunted down, and put to death,' swore Pentecost.

Without a word the twenty-four Mob members rose to gather together. Pentecost was pulled into their midst. There was a firm clasping of paws. 'The oath is bound, and binding unto death,' they roared in unison. Quickly they parted, and with lunch and business over, filed out through the alcove into the outer cellar. Seeing the forlorn look on Pentecost's face, the Scout took him aside. 'You will realise, Decoy, there are many rival Mobs in the city. They would dearly like to learn our food sources and raiding methods. The oath is to ensure that no member of the Gas Street Mob deserts to another gang, for the information he carried could mean our extinction. Should one of us turn traitor, the death penalty would be ruthlessly upheld. It is no idle threat. I tell you this not because I like you more and more, but because a new member should know exactly where he stands.'

'I would never desert to a rival Mob,' said Pentecost hotly. 'I will carry out my duties with honour. But if I can, I will escape at the first opportunity. Surely that is not breaking the oath, for the secrets of the Mob would be little use to my family on Lickey Top.'

'I didn't hear that,' said the Scout, looking cautiously about. 'Not that my sudden deafness is a sign of warmth towards you. I understand your longing for your true home. I will not help, but neither will I hinder your escape. And if you succeed, never imagine that I will miss you from time to time. I was born to pass coldly through life, my honour unsullied. To reach out in friendship is to take sides, and that I cannot do.'

'I didn't hear that,' replied Pentecost, warmly. 'For I feel you are bursting with friendship, inside. . . . ' His words trailed away as the Scout stiffened, turned, and went to stand in lonely silence in a corner of the cellar.

'We are waiting, Decoy Third Class,' bellowed Zero impatiently. 'There is a raid on tonight, I hope you know. You will need to learn what is required of you. The senior Decoy will explain, and then we'll have a practice run.'

With a start Pentecost realised that the Mob had been waiting for him. While he had been pondering the words of the Scout, Zero had been growing angrier, as he called the day-dreaming mouse for the second, third time. Quickly Pentecost hurried to join them. The Sneak was looking pleased. Seniority shone out of him as he strutted up to his junior.

'Now then,' he said. 'Our job . . . no, your job will be to entice Black Shadow, or any other enemies we meet, away from the main raiding-party. This sounds dangerous, and believe me, it is. In other words you will be a set-up patsy. The idea is to stand in a frighteningly open space, and beneath the brightest street-lamp you can find. You should also make as much noise as possible. The result of this stupidity will be for the enemy to immediately attack you. In the meantime, the Carriers and the Breakers will be able to work undisturbed. You are allowed to run, of course, but only when it's almost too late . . . dear God, I'm sweating at the thought of it . . . I myself always broke the rules, and gave myself a good minute's start. It's amazing how one tends to break and run prematurely. You may be required to repeat this luring task three or four times during a raid. Not surprisingly, at the end of the night you will be a complete nervous wreck. After a few days of this nightmarish job, you will begin to dream up cunning plots to shop your friends. You won't care a fig for codes of conduct. You won't care in the least that you have become a feared and despised mouse . . . and you'll creep and crawl and suck up to the powerful, knowing all the time that your life-expectancy is slipping away. God, how I hated that job . . . and the honourable mice wonder why I attempt to frame 'em? They must be joking.' The Sneak was looking wild-eyed and cornered, as he re-lived his terrible experiences.

'Control yourself,' snapped Zero. This was the moment he had been waiting for. He had been thwarted in his efforts to have Pentecost Black-Shadowed, but no-one would be allowed to stop the beating he was about to dish out to that mouse. So he'd come to the city to overthrow folk, had he? Well, he, Zero, could over-throw with the best of them. For accidents would happen. He had got rid of the Chosen mouse, let's see if he couldn't finish this other threat to his vicious rule. He explained what he had in mind.

'I think we should have a little practice run. I will pretend to be Black Shadow, the new member will be the pretend Decoy. Are you ready?'

Pentecost stepped warily into the pool of light that shone in through the hole in the wall. Motionless, he watched as Zero began to stalk across the floor, hissing from the side of his mouth. Suddenly 'Black Shadow' froze and crouched. His tail began to swish from side to side, and his eyes shone evilly as he pretended to catch sight of Pentecost. Immediately he sprang into action. In one great bound he was across the cellar. There was no pretence in his eyes as he confronted a frozen Pentecost. His hate was real, and his quarry was suddenly in no doubt that his life was at stake. Zero would surely have done his victim some dreadful harm, but for Pentecost's prompt action. Swiftly he shot out a defending paw, catching the other flush in the eye. Zero yelled in pain as Pentecost, his fighting blood roused, snatched at the leader's tail, drawing blood as he sank his teeth deep into it. For good measure he stamped as hard as he could on Zero's paws, causing him to hop cursing about the cellar, nursing in turn his eye, tail, and throbbing toes. For a while the Mob stood in shocked silence. Then some began to giggle. The bully-mice just stood looking dumbly on. They watched uneasily as Zero limped

over to where a rivulet of water streamed down the wall. Aided by the crawler Sneak, he began tenderly to bathe his injuries.

'I didn't mean it,' said Pentecost, horrified by the damage he had inflicted. He was as surprised as any that he was capable of such ferocity. The one-eyed mouse was gazing at him with a new respect and admiration.

'Just as well you didn't,' the Breaker commented drily. 'I think Zero has met his match in you. But beware, you have humiliated our leader and he will never forget it. From this moment on you must consider yourself a marked mouse and be constantly on your guard. I and a few friends would like to help, but much as we hate Zero, there is no-one amongst us with those qualities of leadership needed to oppose him. Unless you are he?' There was hope in the eye of the one-eyed mouse.

'Not I,' Pentecost replied, with regret. 'I was told by an old prophet that I would meet with such a mouse, here in the city. He it is who is destined to attempt the overthrow of the tyrant. But I fear the Old Codger's gift proved only part correct. Zero is surely the tyrant mentioned, but of my brave soul-mate there is no sign. I, though a leader in my own peaceful land, am not destined to be one here. I am just a foolish mouse who deserted his family to rush off on a wild-goose chase. Now I am just a marked mouse, and afraid like you.'

The one-eyed mouse sighed. Just then Zero, led by the fussing Sneak, came limping across to the Mob. His left eye was completely closed, while his mutilated tail dragged limply along the ground. To salvage a little of the leader's pride, the Sneak had concocted a most unlikely explanation for the wounds received.

'Zero is such a sure-pawed mouse as a rule,' he mused, shaking his head in puzzlement. 'Yet they accidentally slipped from under him, causing multiple injuries. And he was so enjoying his play-acting with the new Decoy. But he hasn't lost his well-known sense of humour. See, even through the waves of pain, he can still sportingly smile.' Zero forced a weak, and craggy-toothed grin. But from his good eye gleamed a pure and savage hatred. Even as the Mob finalised their plans for the coming cheese-raid, that eye never left Pentecost. If looks could kill, the country mouse was dead and buried.

A few minutes later found the Mob lying around the cellar catching forty winks. They would need to be fully

rested and alert for the night's operation. Some moaned
in their sleep, disturbed by the sound of a voice crackling
with anger. It was Zero bawling out his bully-
mice. He was calling them all kinds of slow-witted
idiots. He was demanding to know why they had stood
around gawping while he was being worked over? If it
happened again they would find themselves tossed on
the scrap-heap . . . and so on, and so on. . . . Pentecost
could not sleep. His thoughts were a confused whirl.
Why hadn't he listened to Fox, and returned home as
advised? Why had he felt compelled to journey to the
city, even against his will? And that which nagged at
him most of all: where was that special mouse he was
meant to meet, and help make the city a better place? He
was not to know that that one was already known to
him. They *had* met, though briefly. They had passed
like ships in the night, each to enact their separate roles
in a single purpose. As Pentecost lay fretting in the Gas
Street cellar, the other was blithely gathering flowers,
and strolling through the Autumn brilliance of the
Lickey Hills, to keep a destined date with Fox of
Furrowfield. . . .

6 Fox is Bushed

From the shiny green hide of an evergreen bush two
eyes peered forth. Tired and drooping, their expression
spelt misery. Fox had met with more disaster during his
slow and painful return to the Lowlands. For once his

luck had almost deserted him. Because of his injuries he had been below par. It was unfortunate that Spot and Fat Billy, two local farm-dogs, had decided to romp over Furrowfields that afternoon. They were surprised that they had been able to close with their old enemy so easily. Only a strong will to live had enabled Fox to finally shake them off. The cost: a badly nipped tail and total exhaustion. But now, safe for a while, he lay panting beneath the bush. Peace and rest was what he needed. He would be denied both.

'He'll be in hiding.' Uncle's voice, loud and scornful, disturbed the dozing fox. 'He could even be under this bush.' The luck of the old mouse was truly amazing, for squinting through the leaves his angry eyes met the dulled gaze of Fox. 'What did I tell you?' he scoffed, turning and beckoning the others.

Soon there were many hostile faces, each taking turn to glare in at their quarry. The bug had flown inside the thick foliage to perch on a leaf above Fox's head. He rapidly summed up the situation. He could tell at a glance that Fox was out on his feet and nearing the end of his tether. This pleased the little insect. Uncle, a blundering mouse, seemed not to notice Fox's condition. But then he was too puffed-up with his own self-importance to consider the feelings of others. He had ordered the Chosen mouse to stay out of sight, to 'lap up more countryside' until needed. Uncle's idea was to spring him on Fox out of the blue. But the timing was vital. The old mouse knew that moments of triumph could be tricky to handle, and a mistimed second either way could ruin them. With a couldn't-care-less shrug, the Chosen mouse had sauntered away to pick more flowers.

'We want an explanation,' insisted Uncle, grimly.

'And no lies, mind, or I'll be in at you paws a-quiver. We demand that you tell us exactly what happened in the city. Begin whenever you wish, Furrowfield.'

Fox raised his aching head and groaned. 'Of all the bushes in the world you have to walk into mine. Is all this necessary? You have the Pentecost mouse back. Why rake over old ground?'

'There is a hole in that argument for a start,' said a triumphant Uncle. 'Carry on, let's see how many more we can pick.

'Very well,' replied Fox weakly. 'If it will get rid of you quicker. The mouse and I arrived in the city. We were exploring a few dustbins when the trouble started. All hell broke loose, and before I knew it the mouse had become swept up by a gang of city mice. They vanished into a hole in a wall.'

'Was he swept willingly?' interrupted Uncle.

'Ask him yourself,' snapped Fox, his patience at an end. 'He's got a tongue in his head. Where is he, by the way? Not that I'm interested.'

'I'm asking the questions,' came Uncle's stern reply. 'I will put it to you again.'

Fox sighed. 'Swept willingly . . . . Not exactly.'

'Did you shout encouragingly down the hole at any time?' continued Uncle, pursing his snout. 'A true friend would surely have done that.'

'I believe I shouted goodbye,' said Fox, attempting a weak joke. Then his temper flared. 'What's this all about? I wish you'd tell me, for frankly I'm baffled.'

Uncle ignored the outburst. 'What happened afterwards?' he persisted. 'You shouted goodbye, then what?'

'If you must know, because I felt like it, I hung around. Then I heard noise and saw a scuffle, and suddenly the little pest came out of the hole again. In fact Black Shadow had scooped him up. Anyway, after a bit of a set-to, I brought him back home. Satisfied?'

'We are not,' shouted Uncle delightedly. His timing was perfect as he turned to yell from the bush, his paws cupped about his snout, 'Hey you, come here.'

After a few moments another head came poking into the bush. Floppy of ear, curious of eye, the mouse stared long and hard at Fox. The sheer insolence took Fox's breath away. After all he had suffered for the Pentecost mouse, and now that one seemed to be pretending not to know him. But the final straw for Fox was to view the linked chain of purple Michaelmas daisies hanging around the mouse's neck, as if he had forgotten his terrible experiences in the city and now hadn't a care in the world. Fox's astonished gaze returned to Uncle, who was jigging impatiently about. At last the old mouse's great moment had come.

'Take a good look, Furrowfield,' he said, trying to contain his jubilation. 'Name this mouse if you can.'

'This has to be a joke,' replied Fox, bewildered. 'Don't you think I know the annoying Pentecost mouse when I see him? Clear off, the lot of you. And before you say any more, I didn't ask him to come to the city, he followed me.'

'Wrong!' cried Uncle. 'This mouse has never been to the city, he only comes from it.'

'And somewhere therein lies a logic of sorts,' broke in the amused bug. 'But don't let me destroy this magical moment. Pray let this farce continue.'

At this point Uncle was almost beside himself with excitement. The words came tumbling from his mouth. 'You didn't bring home the Pentecost mouse, you brought back the Chosen one, instead!' he bellowed.

'Did you think you could fool us with a good copy? Well you didn't hoodwink me for one second.'

'He did, but we'll let that pass,' said the gleeful bug, hugging himself. He cocked an eye at Fox. 'And your reply?'

'Chosen mouse?' Fox was floundering now. 'What's the old fool on about? Chosen by whom, and for what? I must warn you I never discuss religion under bushes. Quit this nonsense for Heaven's sake. Anyone can see he is the Pentecost mouse.'

'Ask him!' bawled Uncle, grabbing the flower-draped mouse by a raggedy ear. 'Ask him who he is, and where he comes from, I dare you!'

'Who are you and where do you come from?' asked a weary Fox. 'And please, no more complications. I did as you wished and took you to the city. I also risked life and limb to rescue you and bring you back. Would I do that if I didn't think a little of you? Even a lot, for I believe our relationship was developing nicely. You've had your adventure, and no one can ever again call you a boring mouse, so why all this aggro? What else do I have to do to prove a loyal friend?'

'You and I, friends?' the Chosen mouse had shrugged

Uncle aside, and was looking at Fox with contempt. 'I am told you dragged me back here unconscious. It was certainly against my will. You also damaged my tail in the process. With friends like you, who needs enemies?'

'Is this really happening to me?' Fox felt both bewildered and angry. 'So why do I stand for it? One sweep of my paw and all my troubles would be over. . . . '

Uncle had backed hastily away. Not so the Chosen mouse. He stood his ground. Shaking a warning paw in Fox's face, he let him have it. 'Before you blow your top I might as well warn you it's a Chosen mouse you are tangling with. I am under the protection of a power that could blow you away with a puff, so spake my old prophet. For one day I am destined to become a leader amongst mice. Though not, I hasten to say, this Lickey Top rabble, for that would be too cruel a joke. And another thing. Don't come all aggrieved with me. Remember, you are just an unimportant large red shape, with only a small walk-on part in my great future. By the way, are those distant hills really blue, or is it just the effect of light and shade . . . ?' He cradled his nose in a paw, and gazed out of the bush at the Clent Hills. He seemed to have lost all interest in the proceedings.

'Well?' shouted Uncle. 'Do you still believe this snappy talker is the Pentecost mouse?'

'Never this side of Christmas,' Fox replied. Surprise was not the only emotion he felt. For that flippant remark concealed a sudden sinking feeling. He was at this moment coming to terms with the fact that he had made a terrible mistake. And with that feeling came an inner despair and sadness. For now the realisation was painfully clear. He had lost a friend, nay abandoned one, to the pitiless city. No matter that he had carried this Chosen mouse home, believing him to be Pentecost. He should have checked, made sure, done all manner of things; and now it was too late and he blamed himself. But he was determined not to betray his feelings. It was obvious the deputation had journeyed from Lickey Top in the hope of watching him eat crow. Well, Fox of Furrowfield would not give them that satisfaction. They would see only an uncaring Fox, the caring one ever tucked away in his secret heart. He spoke on. 'So, it appears I risked my life for a complete stranger? And an extremely obnoxious one, too?'

'I knew you'd slip up one of these days,' smirked the bug. 'I've been waiting for this for a long time.'

'So what is he going to do about it?' demanded Uncle, glaring fiercely at Fox. 'I say the sooner he snatches up this double by the tail, doubles to the city, nips up the real Pentecost, dashes back to Lickey Top, the sooner he'll get his breath back.'

'And while you get yours back I'll tell you this,' snapped Fox. 'So I made a mistake. But the Pentecost mouse made a greater one. I begged him to stay home where he belonged.'

'That is a lie!' bellowed Uncle, his whiskers quivering with rage. 'Why, you practically dragged that poor mouse off to the city, according to this witness cockle-snorkle.'

'And dragged me back in his place,' chimed in the bitter Chosen mouse. 'I realise now I was meant to come, but I was hoping for a smoother ride. Frankly, beautiful though it is, this place is beginning to give me the pip. And these nutcase harvest mice don't help matters.'

'I can still see that sordid little scene,' said the bug, pretending horror. 'In my mind's eye I can still see the Pentecost mouse being dragged away to the city, his cries for help getting fainter and weaker . . . .'

'Rubbish,' growled Fox. 'Who's fool enough to believe a word you say?'

'I am,' said Uncle. 'But I am prepared to overlook that cruel act if you and the Chosen mouse obey my instructions.' He addressed the Chosen mouse, distaste in his voice. 'As you have run up the city, and run down Lickey Top ever since you arrived, we are going to pack you off back to where you belong. The bonus for us will be to see the back of you, and the front of the returning Pentecost. Now, as you and Fox are in this up to your necks, you must work together to solve this problem. As you know the city so well I am ordering Fox to ask you many searching questions. This information will stop him bumping into walls and falling down holes that he thought weren't there when he arrives in the city on his dangerous rescue attempt. So pay attention, for Fox is anxious to bound to his feet and become a blur of speed upon the horizon. Is that not so, Furrowfield?'

'Not quite,' replied Fox drily. 'I much prefer the peace of this bush for the time being.'

'You refuse to question this mouse?' snapped Uncle. 'You wish to be left in peace instead?'

'I think you've just about summed it up,' said Fox, with a yawn, keeping up the pretence that he couldn't care less.

'I wouldn't have answered anyway,' butted in the Chosen mouse. 'He hasn't said sorry for damaging my tail.'

'So neither of you will budge an inch?' said Uncle, stroking his snout and trying to appear wise. In fact, he was completely out of his depth. He was too slow to realise that he was heading for a dead end of his own making. But he struggled on, trying to make sense of his own words. Then he neatly trapped himself. 'So we might as well go home, then? We are wasting our time?'

'Right on, don't let me keep you,' encouraged Fox. In fact all he wished for was to be left alone to plan the rescue of his friend in his own way.

But he too fell into his own trap. His next remarks were pounced upon by Uncle who was desperately trying to figure out what to do next. 'And don't forget to take the Chosen mouse with you,' Fox said. 'I wouldn't say it before, but, my, does he pong of bad drains.' Eagerly Uncle looked around for the Chosen mouse who had wandered out of the bush. It seemed the city mouse had developed a passion for the brightly coloured Autumn leaves that lay scattered about. Upon Uncle's command he crawled back, a wad of them clutched tightly to his puny chest.

'Do you know you are offending Fox's nose?'

'I resent that remark,' came the indignant reply. 'What's wrong with a whiff of motorway fumes, and over-ripe cheddar? And am I responsible for the drainage in the city?'

'You can resent all you like,' grimaced Uncle. 'You and Furrowfield must settle your differences and plan your rescue of the Pentecost mouse. Do you think I at my age can remain in charge on Lickey Top for ever? So you will take a bath in the brook. Then, when you return fresh and clean, Furrowfield will say he is sorry about your tail. You can then embrace, and begin to hit it off.'

'A brilliant idea,' grinned the bug.

'I've never taken a bath in my life,' said the Chosen mouse proudly. 'Let it go on record, this liquid refreshment will be taken under protest.'

Uncle then spoke to a sighing Fox. 'We will go and dip the Chosen mouse in the brook. Be here when we return.'

'In living colour,' Fox promised. 'I swear not to move a muscle.'

'He hardly being able to,' explained the all-knowing bug. 'How I wish I could admire the gallant way Fox hides his suffering, what with his city wounds, and his maddened dash from those tail-nipping dogs. But then my spirit was never generous. But come, let us away to the babbling brook, for watching fools at play is a hobby of mine.' So saying, he sped off in the direction of the waters; the mice, with the Chosen mouse under close escort, following along behind.

Fox winced as he eased an aching paw. He settled down to enjoy what little peace he could, and to gather together all the facts so far in his mind. He no longer doubted the prophecy of the Old Codger, for the pieces were slipping comfortably into the unfinished jig-saw: Pentecost's role, his own as the 'large red shape', and that of the Chosen mouse. *Exactly* where he fitted Fox was not yet sure, but he would find out in his own good time. He still could not quite get over the astonishing likeness the two mice shared. Though as for their personalities, they were as chalk and cheese. Not a likeable mouse at all, the Chosen One. Not like . . . again Fox felt a deep sadness well up inside. Urgency was the key-word; that was, if Pentecost still lived. Fox shrugged that thought away and hoped, and hoped again. And still he blamed himself. He had made a terrible mistake in identity – or was it meant to be? Uneasiness fluttered in Furrowfield's heart. Anger, too. He had always placed great value on his freedom to come and go as he pleased. The thought that fate was manipulating him came as a heavy blow. The knowledge that some mysterious influence was pulling the strings, humbling him to the role of a mere puppet, dented his pride. Confused, annoyed, yet curious too, Fox awaited the return of the bathing party. He had, indeed, certain questions to put to the Chosen mouse. . . .

Meanwhile, that mouse was undergoing a new experience. Upon arriving at the brook, Uncle had rapped out an order. Immediately the victim was seized by his floppy ears and dunked into the cold, swift flow. After what seemed an age he was hauled spluttering to the surface. Though half-drowned, he was as cheeky as ever. Sporting, too. He was determined that these sissy mice would not see the distress he really felt.

'I am beginning to feel like a new mouse already,' he gasped. 'I must say, I am really enjoying this wash and brush-up. Hey –' Again the waters received him. Grimly and aloud, Uncle counted off long seconds, adding an extra five for good measure. Streaming wet and gulping for air, still the spirit of the Chosen mouse was undaunted.

'Third time lucky,' he gurgled. 'For suddenly I feel this to be a test. All at once the urge to bathe is strong in me. . . .'

Uncle's assistants obliged. At long last the Chosen mouse, cleansed to within an inch of his life, was dumped upon the grassy bank to drain off and recover. Bemused, his head in a whirl, he was content to just lie there, his brown and white fur steaming in the late afternoon sun. And as he dried, so a feeling of well-being overcame him. It was quite unexpected, for he and water had never got on. Yet really, it felt not half-bad to be clean. Then with a start he thought back to the words of the old prophet: ' . . . there you will be cleansed inside and out, that you may be humbled to learn many lessons. . . . ' Could all that unpleasant ducking be what the old hedgehog had meant? Unpleasant, for despite his jokey acceptance of it, he had hated every moment. But then perhaps a Chosen mouse was required to be clean? After all, it was but a small price to pay for being so honoured. Then the realisation dawned. Honoured . . . until now he had never regarded himself so. Lucky, certainly, for hadn't his new status kept the wrath of Zero at bay? With growing alarm he began to see responsibilities looming ahead. For the first time the real import of his destiny came home to him. He, from birth always considered a hopeless case, ever fearful of authority, had had thrust upon him the task he was least equipped for. In fact, to depose the one he secretly feared above all others? And when that time came, all the flip, the smart-alec quips, the false bravado, would help him not at all. And he knew he could not do it. *Would* not do it.

'Are you going to lie there all day?' Uncle was glaring down, his face set and angry. 'Up on those idle paws. Furrowfield is anxiously waiting us.'

That was not true. But Uncle had always assumed too much. Fox was groaning as he listened to the sound of hastily returning paws. Once more the leaves of the bush were parting, and for one brief moment Fox wished he had never been born. Why, he agonised, did that old mouse annoy him so? It was a foolish question.

'Now wrinkle you nose,' challenged Uncle. 'I want you to repeat after me: "Dear Chosen mouse, please accept my humble and sincere apologies for the pain I caused your tail." You will then lower your meek nose and eyes to the ground.'

'Forget it,' growled Fox. 'I'm sorry, and that's his lot.'

'Couldn't memorise it all, eh?' smirked Uncle. 'It will be old age. I have noticed a few wrinkles around your jowls. Very well, as you two are now close friends, you can begin to question and answer each other.' He lowered his skinny haunches onto a fallen twig, and spreading his paws, prepared to tick off important points as they arose. The Chosen mouse, his fur dry and glowing like silk, gazed up at Fox. The bug, all lemon-bright, obligingly cast his light upon the proceedings, ears craned so as not to miss a word. The small mice, unable to squeeze into the already packed bush, pushed and shoved for a good view inside, from outside.

'First of all, let's get one thing straight,' began Fox. 'I would like it to go on record that I am an unwilling party to all this destiny thing. However, as the Pentecost mouse is in dire need I will agree to help. But I have a choice, you understand. I could walk from this bush, and nothing and nobody could stop me.'

'But you won't, eh, Fox?' said the bug slyly. 'Like me, you are beginning to realise there is more in this destiny business than meets the eye. I myself am plotting my own role to play. But then no doubt, I will receive some divine call, sooner or later – '

Fox cut him short. Eyeing the Chosen mouse, he said, 'What happens to you is of no concern to me. My object is to return the Pentecost mouse to his family. Also in that way I can get this irritating old Uncle mouse off my back.'

'And a fine help you'll be,' retorted the Chosen mouse. 'If every time you hear a twig snap you dive under a bush, I don't see much hope for this Pentecost.'

Fox ignored the insult. 'I admit there has been a

mix-up, and I have somehow become involved. But then I knew there'd be trouble, allowing that Old Codger and Son onto Lickey Top.'

'Tell us how you intend to unravel it all!' shouted Uncle. 'Never mind about shifting the blame to my friend the Old Codger. Why haven't you asked questions and set off for the city at once? How much longer must we bear the jokes of the drily-cracking Chosen mouse? As deputy leader of the family I insist that you do your duty, and bring home the correct mouse, dead or alive.'

'Could he still be alive?' asked Fox of the Chosen One. 'Was he alive when you left?'

The Chosen mouse shrugged. 'Just about. But I don't reckon his chances. His mouth will do for him. For a start he got the Scout off the hook by offering an eye-witness account. Zero hated that. Then he boasted about being a leader in his own land. That was fatal. Zero won't tolerate rivals. That's why he tried to do for me. Heaven knows what he's said since. Alive . . . I suppose there's a slim chance.'

'But a chance, nevertheless?' mused Fox.

'Action is what is needed,' fumed Uncle. 'Talk, talk, that's all you do, Furrowfield. Well, I'm not staying here to listen to it. I have important things to do. My final words are that Furrowfield must never set paw on Lickey Top without the Pentecost mouse dangling from his jaws. If that approaching Furrowfield does not wink, we will fear the worst. In that event, a small, sadly-scuffed hole will be waiting for our leader beneath Owl's tree.' So saying, he scrambled out of the bush.

'So now you've been told,' chuckled the bug. He glanced down at Fox and the Chosen mouse. 'I think I'll nip into the city and see what's going on. Of course, if I were a good little bug, I would return and put you in the picture. But then if I came back and told you the Pentecost mouse was alive or dead, you wouldn't believe a word of it. And why should you? I'm just not to be trusted. So enjoy your meaningful relationship. See you sometime. . . . ' He sped from the bush. Instantly the interior became dark and gloomy.

'This is how a bush should be,' said Fox to himself. 'Empty.'

Suddenly, unexpectedly, something was draped upon his nose. A surprised Fox lowered his eyes to view a chain of purple flowers swinging there. A gift, a peace-offering – yet quickly observing, Fox saw the twinkle in the eye of the Chosen mouse. There was a wariness there too; but a promise of future friendship, perhaps? Maybe, maybe not. Though one thing was certain. Like it or lump it, fate had thrown them together. Whether in stony silence or true companionship, they would journey to the city together. In the meantime they settled down for the night. Strangers still, yet the truce between them was at least a step along that long road.

7 King and the Basin Swingers

The Scout First Class had hurried across to the hole in the wall. For a while he stood peering out into the darkness, his whiskers fluttering in the chill breeze sweeping down the alley-way. He returned. 'I can't see him about,' he said. 'But I'll check behind the bins, just in case.' Again he approached the hole. This time he vanished outside.

'Can't you feel your bones turning to jelly?' mouthed the Sneak. 'Just think, Black Shadow could be crouched in hiding out there.'

Pentecost was unable to reply. He was trembling, his mouth dry with fear as he wondered what awaited them out in the streets. Yet he felt excitement, too. For once embarked upon the cheese-raid, he intended to give the Mob the slip and escape if he could. To where, he had no idea as yet. But foremost in his mind was the hope that he might recognise some feature in the city. For the way in must also be the way out of this awful place, if he could only find it. Now if Fox was here with his tracking skills . . . but he wasn't. He had deserted when the going got rough, thought Pentecost, bitterly. He could not know how unfair this thinking really was. But such was his mental state he was prepared to blame anyone for the mess he was in.

'Don't worry,' whispered the Sneak, noticing the shivers that ran through the small frame of his junior. 'Remember and take comfort: I will be keeping an eye on you from the protecting shadows. If you see something scrunched against a wall, it will be me watching you, watching me.'

Meanwhile the Scout had reappeared. His brief nod indicated the way was clear. Softly, the Scout leading the way, the Mob slipped out into the alley in single file. Zero and his bully-mice bringing up the rear. Grim of face, the leader had more than cheese on his mind that night. Before the dawn broke a certain country mouse would be no more. He allowed himself a thin smile as he savoured the thought. Then, on and on through the bright light and dark shades of the city; not too far behind, a slinking shape, green eyes a-glitter, padded silently along in their wake. . . .

There were other Mobs out that night. The Queensway raiding party hurried by, going the other way. The Broad Street Mob, their Scouts out ahead and scanning the line of advance, surged across the path of the Gas Street Mob. No greetings, no words were exchanged. Just the odd suspicious glance, for each band had their own secret cheese sources, jealously guarded. Now the breathless mice, Pentecost stumbling in their midst, were dashing across a roaring, shaking road, cut and slashed by needles of light. Safe over, coughing as they fought to clear their lungs from fumes, they were soon bowling across a vast paved expanse, dotted with trussed-up and sickly looking shrubs. Now the Gas Street Mob could see their destination. Quickly they gained the shadows of a multi-windowed block, thankfully diving into the refuse that littered its frontage. The Scout had more work to do. Flitting along the cluttered pavement, he suddenly vanished.

'Put that Decoy out,' snarled Zero, from the side of his mouth. He was addressing the cowering Sneak. There was no need to ask twice. Viciously, the Sneak grabbed Pentecost and hurried him out to stand alone in that naked place so recently crossed, his sole companion, a drenching pool of light from a lamp above. The Sneak then gambolled back to safety.

'If that's not the brightest light in the world,' he hissed, nudging Zero, 'I think I'll award myself another credit mark for initiative. And now, if you don't mind, my leader . . . .' He crept beneath a cardboard box and crouched, his eyes peering fearfully about.

The Scout returned. 'It's a job for the Breakers,' he whispered. 'We'll never get the loot out through that gap.'

Zero rapped out an order. Obediently, two strong-jawed Breakers, one First the other Second Class, emerged from cover to follow the Scout to the door he had found. Quickly they set to work enlarging the way in, chips of rotting wood flying and piling up behind them.

Zero and his bullies had joined the Sneak in his cardboard box. As the rest of the Mob got on with their different tasks, the cowardly five seemed to be enjoying a private joke. Now and then they would point towards where a small mouse shook and shivered beneath the harsh street light.

'Send in the Carriers!' came a harsh voice. A Breaker came skidding to a halt, blowing and sneezing from the wood-dust clinging to his nose and whiskers. Proudly, between throaty hawks, he added: 'We only broke through in record time, didn't we?'

Half a dozen Carriers had dashed from hiding to disappear beneath the hole in the door. Soon they came squeezing back out, their paws loaded down with crumbs of cheese. Zero sniffed, and looked disappointed. 'Foreign rubbish,' he grumbled. 'Oh well, stack it, and get back for more. And hurry.'

The arrival of the next precious load coincided with the arrival of Black Shadow. The Scouts, ears ever to

the ground, had picked up the familiar click, click of claws upon the pavement. Instantly they were shouting warnings to the mice still inside the store. Then everyone was assisting the Carriers to snatch up the precious booty, before making off at full speed. Scattering to confuse the great cat, each mouse made his independent way homewards. Only the Scout First Class spared a thought for the hapless and flood-lit Pentecost.

'Run out of the light,' he shouted. 'Follow me. It's advice, understand, not a kindness.' Then he too had gone.

For a moment Pentecost stood transfixed. He seemed hypnotized as he watched Black Shadow spinning this way and that, hissing and lashing out in an attempt to cut off the fleeing mice. Then he was spotted. The sleek, green-eyed shape crouched, his claws making eager cuffing movements as he sidled across the paving stones towards his prey. It was sheer primitive instinct that shook Pentecost from his frozen state. He was off and away, taking advantage of every scrap of cover, ducking and diving, Black Shadow ever close behind. Once he was caught and rolled. Frantically he somehow twisted free, regained his paws and dashed on, not knowing where his flight led him. Then from the corner of a desperately seeking eye he recognised a land-mark – then another. After what seemed an eternity, he was bowling down a Gas Street alley; not that one he had set out from, but who cared? Now his chest was threatening to burst, but he plunged on, colliding with tin-cans, slipping on garbage, and then he was skidding to a halt. Too late. Into the murky waters of the canal he plunged, leaving behind on the shore a yowling Black Shadow, frustrated beyond measure. Hardly a swimmer, the terrified mouse bravely struck out for he knew not where. . . .

'I hate to see . . . that evening sun go down . . . '
sang a soulful voice, the notes echoing along the Gas
Street Basin. The singer was accompanied by a melodious humming, sweet upon the ear.

The half-drowned swimmer saw the rope trailing in
the water. He clutched at it, gasping and coughing oily
water from his lungs.

'I hate to see . . . the evening sun go down . . . ' the
words of the song were repeated even more plaintively.
The close harmony hummers seemed equally moved.

Inch by painful inch, Pentecost hauled himself up the
slimy rope, the filthy canal water cascading from his
tail. The 'sun going down' song ended on a note of
sadness. Yet in those voices was a lustiness that suggested a great love of music. The song, though sad, was for
happy singers sung with much taste and feeling.

Now Pentecost had scaled the rope and was thankfully
hoisting himself up and over, onto a smooth wet
surface. The opening bars of a fresh song trailed away
into silence.

'Hi,' hailed a voice. 'If you're a tenor, welcome
aboard.' Pentecost tried to stand and slipped heavily, the
shock of falling causing him to cry out loud.

'That's a tenor,' said another, satisfied voice. 'A mite
strangled perhaps, but with training . . . praise the
Lord, the Basin Swingers Trio are now a quartet.'

'God send an applauding audience and our happiness
will be complete,' cried another. Apprehensively, Pentecost approached the shadowy strangers. There were
three in all, the one in the centre towering above his
companions.

'We could stand him in front of King,' suggested one
of the side-kicks. 'In that way our act would achieve a
balance pleasing to the eye, don't you think?'

'But what if he's tone-deaf?' said the other. 'What if he doesn't know a top C from his elbow?'

'So hopes are dashed,' replied the right side-kick, shrugging. They continued to converse, eyeing Pentecost with interest as he slithered across the deck towards them. Somehow he managed the trip. Soon he had halted, and was looking up at them in nervous anticipation.

'Perhaps the small artist would agree to an audition?' said the large, central water-rat, his voice shy, and hesitant. He spoke very deeply. It was the kind of voice that seemed to be singing when it wasn't. It was also, thought a relieved Pentecost, a warm-sounding one. King, for that was his name, continued. 'Perhaps if we gave him a key, he would give us a C in return? In that way he shouldn't fly into a primadonna tantrum?'

'A sort of exchange system?' agreed the left side-kick. 'That sounds fair enough.'

Anxiety filled the mouse. He had no idea what a C was. Surely he would not be denied refuge because of something he did not possess? He tried to explain. He had arrived in such haste, he said, and had quite forgotten to bring along a C. He wasn't as a rule a forgetful mouse, and he could only humbly apologise for his bad manners.

'You've probably caught a frog in the throat,' said the right side-kick, sympathizing. 'But what do you expect, gargling with canal water? Never mind, we'll take five. Give the pipes time to clear, eh?'

Pentecost's heart sank still further. Now they wanted five C's. He decided to throw himself on their mercy. 'The truth is, I came here empty-pawed and wringing wet,' he blurted. 'I was escaping from Black Shadow, and the five C's completely slipped my mind. I'm sorry, I truly am.'

'We meant take five minutes rest,' grinned the right side-kick. He looked at Pentecost quizzically. 'New to the music scene, are we?'

'Very,' the mouse confessed. 'But I'm a quick learner if you decided to let me stay.' He gazed at them appealingly. Their silence prompted him to explain his situation. 'You see, I'm a simple country mouse, lost in the city. I came on a sacred mission, but alas, fell in with the Gas Street Mob. Since then, fate has not treated me kindly. . . . ' And with his voice breaking from time to time, he poured out his story to the quietly listening Basin Swingers. It took a long while, and meantime it began to get light.

The Gas Street Basin was a hive of tunnels and arches through which snaked the placid waters of the canal. Brightly-painted narrow-boats squatted along both banks. The waters were black, but sometimes silver where the light squeezed through. Here and there an oily rainbow shone, casting riotous reflections on the dripping, blue-brick walls. The scene, so quiet and still, was reminiscent of a penny post-card from a bygone age.

The water-rats had not interrupted as Pentecost's troubles unfolded. Yet strangely, they seemed uninterested in the fact that he feared for his life. The mouse soon realised that even had all the devils in Hell been on his tail, it would have made small impression upon the trio. But yes, they admitted, they knew Zero and the Mob very well. 'We have approached them many times,' said the sad, right side-kick. 'But always they turn our offers down.'

'We have even sat outside their cellar, practising scales to tempt them, but to no avail,' joined in his friend.

'Perhaps they have no rythm in their souls?' concluded

King. 'If only they would listen to a few bars their fierceness would subside. . . . '

'A snatch of blues to set them swaying,' agreed the right side-kick.

'Perhaps they have no music in their toes?' finished King. 'Often, toes that cannot tap seek mischief.'

'Mine tap perfectly,' said Pentecost, eager to please. He went further. Without more ado he sang them a ballad from the hills, his voice clear and strong. And the water-rats joined in, blending beautifully, for music came naturally to them. Only then, after the mouse had proved his lyric worth, did the trio express a half-hearted interest in his problems.

'Perhaps this Fox of Furrowfield will return for you,' said King. 'Chances are he will not be able to help himself, for a poet is the staunchest of friends. Anyway, until his return you will stay here with us, and make music?'

Pentecost felt strangely uncomfortable as King gazed down at him. It was as if the other saw deep into his soul. King raised his eyes once more, the early morning light playing full upon his face. It was then Pentecost, very humbled, realised that the large water-rat was quite blind. He who hated to see the sun go down, saw nothing through those white-filmed eyes. The mouse whispered his regrets, apologising for not having noticed before. The right side-kick hastened to put him at ease. Proudly the small rat looked up at their singer. He had been blind from birth, he explained. But hadn't God been moved to compensate him with the gift of song? And though he could not see the sun go down, he could feel its warmth passing across his face. 'Though not golden, yet still beautiful,' chimed the left side-kick. 'For inside he is gifted with the colour of feeling. And gold was never so bright that mere eyes could see. Feel sorrow for yourself, small mouse, for King is home and feels it – you are lost and sadly see it.'

'Amen,' murmured King, in his deep bass voice. 'Perhaps one finds happiness in the shadows of the world.'

'So let us speak of happy things.' The right side-kick was all cheeriness.

'Like how glad we are that we now have a contralto to form our quartet,' said his comrade.

'The tenor of your voice being higher than we thought,' explained the other, kindly. 'We have long considered expanding, trios being so unfashionable these days. A new look will surely bring the fickle crowds flocking in.'

Pentecost looked surprised. 'But don't they flock in already?' he asked. 'For myself I would be first in the queue, and easily the loudest clapper.'

'Ah, to perform before a multitude . . . .' The reply was filled with longing. 'In all our long career we have never performed before an audience. Our lives have been but one long cancelled date ever since we formed together. But fame surely awaits us if only someone will bend an ear . . . . Our only hope lies in a fresh start. As quartets are so "in" these days, would you give the matter serious thought?'

'I have, and I accept the contralto slot,' said Pentecost promptly.

'Lowly buskers are booed quite often,' cautioned the right side-kick. 'For us, the big time may hide around many corners. . . .'

'Real stardom might remain forever a will-o'-the-wisp,' warned his friend. 'But then that's Show Business.'

'Anything is better than being a Decoy in the Gas Street Mob,' replied Pentecost, vastly relieved. 'For Zero, who hates me, will surely say I broke the oath by deserting. Though I didn't. I will gladly help you to wow the world. In the meantime I will live in hope that Fox will pluck up the courage to return for me.'

'I have a brilliant idea,' said the excited right side-kick. 'As our old trio was always getting snubbed and chucked out of gigs, we will try a new gimmick. We will send ahead the new contralto. He can warble a few high notes to whet the appetites of the punters – .'

'Then we will burst in to join in sudden harmony!' whooped his partner. 'And once inside the joint, we will slay them with the blues.'

King squeezed shut his sightless eyes as if to hold back tears. It was as if he could see in his mind's eye the enthusiastic crowds, refusing the quartet pause to rest hoarse and happy throats.

'Though never for King the up-turned and enraptured faces,' cried the left side-kick, 'yet a tumult of praise in his ears, yelling "Encore . . . encore!" Such will be his reward.'

'Encore!' yelled an exultant Pentecost, his own troubles for the moment forgotten. King smiled, and fumbling, found and patted the mouse about his mis-shapen ears. 'If King lived on Lickey Top he would be cheered all day long,' went on Pentecost loyally. As he said the words so a wave of nostalgia overcame him. The mention of his own beloved home, perhaps forever lost to him, was more than he could bear.

King seemed to sense the mouse's mood. 'There, there,' he consoled. 'Perhaps the red poet and his blue friend will meet again one day.'

'As surely as fame awaits the quartet out in the city,'

agreed a confident right side-kick. Then ominously, 'Even though we would be very reluctant to lose our new contralto.'

The future significance of that remark was lost on Pentecost. All he knew was that he felt safe and amongst friends.

'But let us not speak of partings,' begged the third water-rat. 'Instead let us sing King's song in celebration.'

And there in the gloomy Basin the newly formed quartet sang the beautiful sun-going-down song, their harmonies cementing a bond of sorts. As they sang so a single shaft of sunlight, piercing in through a crack in the echoing arches, lit up their happy faces. None of them noticed that for the last choruses or so they were a quintet, for thus did the extra voice make them. Amusedly singing along was a bright orange bug. He had no problem with the words and tune, for he had been listening and watching for quite some time. He wasn't half-bad a singer he thought, sort of pleased. But music was not his passion. Melodies were all right for quartets, but mischief was his first and only love. Glancing at that seeping ray of sunshine, he correctly gauged the time to be around midday. So what next? Should he first return to upset the harvest mice of Lickey Top, or would a trip to the Lowlands best suit his purpose? He decided to make up his mind on the way home. He rose to zip across the canal. Soon he was winging up the Gas Street alley, and then up, up, out of the city, into the open countryside. . . .

8 Time for Learning

Fox had been enjoying a quiet chicken breakfast when the Chosen mouse crawled out of the bush to disturb him. Famished, the mouse had risked a quick lick at a discarded bone, only to shrink away in distaste. Since that time Fox had had to listen to a constant string of complaints and insults. He was not fooled for a moment. Indeed, Fox of Furrowfield had weighed up the Chosen mouse long ago. Brash, cheeky, the tiny creature had hang-ups which stuck out a mile. But Fox, absently licking chicken grease from his paws, decided not to broach the subject. He guessed confession time was fast approaching. Idly he watched the mouse foraging for something to appease his hunger. With a grimace, the mouse nibbled upon a few grass-seeds and a sweet-root – a bland diet indeed for someone brought up on tangy cheese. Fox's comments didn't help matters. Quietly needling, he soon had the mouse in a fine old temper. Shrewdly, Fox judged the other was ready to crack. A few more well chosen words would do the trick.

'Aren't we the hard-boiled one?' he remarked. 'But then, what can we expect from a tough city nut? By the way, there'll be no time to link daisy-chains this morning. The sun is shining, the birds are chirping their little throats raw, it's a perfect morning for not being here. Come on, small mouse, we have a long journey in front of us.'

'So brave, aren't you?' sneered the mouse. 'Where's the hurry? The city won't run away.'

'There speaks one worried mouse,' said Fox. 'And I thought you were raring to go? I think it's come-clean time, don't you?'

It was. The Chosen mouse was suddenly subdued. No longer cocky and indignant, he seemed to shrink. His eyes had a strange haunted look. His flop-eared dejected slump told its own tale. Here was a mouse with a shaming problem, until now firmly suppressed and hidden from the world. For a long time he remained silent. Yet it was obvious to Fox that a fierce struggle was taking place within that small breast, and, aware of the other's distress, he spoke kindly. His words had the desired effect. The barrier broke and crumbled.

'Let's be honest with each other,' Fox encouraged. 'Get it off your chest. You'll feel better for it.'

'What do you know of fear?' blurted the Chosen mouse in bitter tones.

'Quite a lot,' was the quiet reply. 'But there comes a time in life when deception doesn't work any more. This is your time. Face yourself, little mouse of destiny. Come on, let it all hang out. . . .'

Sympathetically listening, he was treated to a review of the mouse's short life. In agonised sentences, the story unfolded. How for as long as he could remember, the mouse had lived in a state of perpetual fear. How he had had the misfortune to be born one of those mice who were crushed in the scramble to secure a safe position in life. But for his wandering on to Spaghetti Junction that day, Zero would surely have disposed of him. At the time, meeting up with the old prophet had seemed a tremendous stroke of luck. By playing upon the super-stitions of Zero and the Mob, he had gained their wary respect. For a few days life had been sweet indeed. All the food he could eat, and never did he need to lift a paw. In his ignorance, he believed that this blissful state of affairs would go on forever. Never for a moment did he pause to consider the grave import of the old hedgehog's words. Only now, after all that had happened, was it beginning to come home to him. Idle, insecure, without apparent talent: nevertheless he of all mice had been chosen to overthrow the tyrant Zero. . . .

'Why me?' he asked despairingly. 'All I ever wanted was to be left alone and unnoticed. A quiet and safe corner in the cellar . . . . Was that too much to ask for?' Thus was revealed the mouse beneath the smart talk, all hung out before the listening fox.

'Ah, to be left alone,' echoed Fox, agreeing as if to comfort. 'How marvellous that sounds. How lucky to be able to crawl into a hole somewhere and blot out the world. But life makes demands, small mouse. Whether you like it or not you have a mission to carry out. And remember, the future happiness of many lives could depend on the decision you must now make. Will you give in to your fear and run, or conquer it? But take heart, you are not alone. Although, I must admit a certain "large red shape" is wishing fate had not dragged him into all this . . . .'

'Now you mock me,' replied the miserable mouse. 'Joke all you want, but your bravery is not in question. You are the mighty Fox of Furrowfield, a genuine hero. Never for you the coward's way out. You won't think twice about risking your life in the city to save a friend. Deep down you must despise me. Deny that you secretly hate the thought of travelling to the city with such as I . . . .'

'I'll tell you a story,' came the reply. 'I know someone

who flees at the snap of a twig, who panics when a leaf falls when there is no wind, who shrinks in the shadows from a too full moon, who starts at the thump of his own quaking heart, who dreads to feel each day that his fate is sealed. . . . '

'His name, the elusive Furrowfield,' finished a derisive voice. It was the bug, hot-wing from the city. He continued, ignoring Fox's vexed groans. 'Perfect afternoon for baring the soul, eh, Fox? You can certainly tell a moving story. I was near to tears at one point. So, all cowards together, are we? After listening to all that, I am astonished that you two found the courage to crawl from beneath that bush.'

Fox stiffened angrily. 'What do you want?'

'You mean, "What do *you* want",' corrected the hovering bug. 'I know I considered leaving you in the dark, but here's some information for you. Ever heard of the Basin Swingers Trio?'

At once the Chosen mouse was all ears. 'You mean the water-rats who live down on the Gas Street canal?'

'The very same,' was the brisk reply. 'This is just to let you know they are now a quartet. A certain refugee Decoy Third Class has swelled their little band. Quite a sweet voice, too.'

'What's this, riddle time?' snapped Fox. 'On your way, trouble-maker.'

'Wait,' shouted the Chosen mouse. He craned back his head as the bug spiralled into the sky, obviously eager to be gone. 'You can't mean the Sneak, he doesn't sing a note. So who *do* you mean?'

'Figure it out for yourself,' yelled the bug, already speeding off in the direction of Lickey Top. 'But hurry, for a certain mouse's singing career will not last long, I'm thinking.' Soon he was but an orange blip, zipping along at tree-top height through the clear blue sky.

'That could mean anything or nothing,' said Fox, irritably. 'I wouldn't trust him as far as I could throw him.'

'He could be taunting us with the truth,' ventured the mouse. 'Liars sometimes do that. Perhaps he is slyly hinting that the Pentecost mouse is still alive. One thing is certain, whoever has joined up with the Basin Swingers, it isn't a member of the Gas Street Mob. No city mouse worth his salt would ever consider singing as a career. City mice detest arty types. Poets in particular, if you'll forgive my saying . . . .'

Fox looked a trifle embarrassed. 'Why should I forgive you?' he asked. But he quickly moved on. 'Well, you are the expert. Could this "refugee Decoy" be the Pentecost mouse, alive and singing?'

'We can live in hope,' was the reply. 'But the proof will only be found in the city – .'

'Hang on,' interrupted Fox, grinning. 'A while ago you were getting ready to duck out, now you're all fired up to go. What brought about this change of heart?'

'If Fox of Furrowfield can triumph over fear, so can the Chosen mouse of Gas Street,' replied the other, sticking out his puny chest. 'I am ready to travel when-ever you are, oh large red shape.'

'Yes, well, first things first,' said Fox, pleased, but trying not to show it. Painfully he got to his feet. Slowly he moved off, not towards the city at all but down to where the sun cast long shadows across the ridges of Furrowfield. The Chosen mouse made to follow him. He was instantly quelled in his tracks by a penetrating look as Fox stopped and turned.

'Ours may be the start of a beautiful friendship,' he said. 'But there is such a thing as privacy. There are areas of my life that are none of your concern, nor ever will be.'

'So where are you going?' asked the surprised mouse. 'Why all the secrecy?'

'Bite your tongue,' was Fox's advice. 'Just wait there until I return. Just sit there and keep repeating over and over again, "I must learn to mind my own business." Have you got that?'

Obediently, the mouse closed his eyes and began to mouth Fox's instructions. But then curiosity overcame him. Through slitted eyes he watched as the other limped off in a peculiar sideways gait, describing a wide and cautious circle. Strange, even funny to watch, yet there was something purposeful about Fox's stealth as he twice crossed that circle before disappearing from view.

As the afternoon lengthened the waiting Chosen mouse had plenty of time to think. He had learned a lot in these past few hours, about himself in particular. He had a lot to thank Fox for. With his help, he had finally faced his own fears. Not that he had banished them. He still dreaded to think of the task that lay before him. But through Fox he had come to realise that the real enemy lay within. Soon, armed with the strength of that knowledge, he would face the enemy without. Win or fail, the trying was all. There, beside the bush, deep in thought, the mouse waited for Fox to return. And soon he did, though neither crackling leaf nor twig betrayed his once again comforting presence. Then it was time to set out. It would be a long and much interrupted meander to the distant city, and mostly passed in silence. For the still lame Fox there would be much pain, but no complaining. Only his snail's pace would betray his suffering. Without speaking, Fox of Furrowfield would, by example, teach the Chosen mouse much about courage. The mouse's respect for the other would increase throughout that journey to the city. Somewhere along the way the wish of the Chosen mouse would be granted, and that respect would be returned in the form of understanding and friendship. . . .

Meanwhile, things on Lickey Top were going from bad to worse. The small mice, looking for someone to look up to, chose Uncle. The old mouse was not displeased. The other more sensible Harvest mice grew more and more worried to see how swiftly the Old Codger and Son were reducing Lickey Top to a shambles. They had learned from Uncle that Fox was on his way to the city to rescue their leader and bring him home. As they gazed hopefully down the hill, willing Pentecost to appear out of the trees at the edge of the Weasel Woods, many harboured harsh thoughts for that mysterious thing called destiny. Was not the world teeming with mice? So why out of them all had their leader been chosen to go haring off to the city just when, they realised it now, he was most needed here on Lickey Top. And to make things worse, the bug had just re turned to inform them that things didn't look too bright in the city. Spitefully, he said that the body of a mouse had been found, and he would be buzzing off to check it out in the morning, so 'paws crossed, eh?' Then he sped off up the hill to check out another suffering soul.

'What do you think of it so far, Owl?' His gimlet eyes peered in at his master. 'I just thought I'd let you know what was going on in the world.'

'What world?' said the bitter bird. 'I've almost forgotten what it looks like. Oh, how I long to glide beneath the stars, over the sparkling Great River. What joy to sink my talons into something soft and juicy. What pleasure to waft gently home and enjoy supper on a moon-lit and tranquil Lickey Top.'

'Sounds heavenly, Owl,' said the bug, concealing a wicked grin. 'Never mind, all things pass. You're just having a bad run of luck, that's all.'

'Bad luck?' whispered the broken bird. 'I've been dogged with bad luck all my life. Bad luck was waiting for me the moment I broke out of my shell.'

'And you've been trying to crawl back into one ever since,' observed the bug, his eyes flicking about the hole's gloomy interior. 'If only your chickhood had been happier . . . .'

'They shout up at me, you know.' A large tear rolled from Owl's saucer-sized eye. 'They know I can't defend myself. Never, "How are you feeling, Owl," but always insults. That old mouse, and the Old Codger and Son . . . they never leave me in peace. And you can see what they've done to Lickey Top.'

'You've always got me, Owl,' comforted the bug. 'I'm only sorry it's always bad news I have to bring. Never mind, you will soon be fit and well again. Then you can sort 'em out. By the way, have you noticed that foot of yours? Not the swollen one, the other . . . oh, deary me, Owl . . . .'

'Oh my God,' groaned the desperate bird, glancing wildly down. 'I was dreading . . . is it swelling up?'

'It's a funny colour,' replied the bug, shaking his head. 'That knuckle's gone purple.'

'And now it's beginning to throb,' yelled Owl hysterically. 'This is like some terrible nightmare. I suspect I can't bear much more of this.'

'But you will bear it bravely I know,' said the bug. 'Only I need a good night's sleep. I have to get up early in the morning. So if you feel the urge to scream out loud, just chuckle instead. It will take your mind off things. So, good-night then, Owl. Sleep tight.' He left the bird grimacing with pain. Soon he had tucked himself away beneath his slip of bark a little way down the trunk of the oak. For a while sleep escaped him. His active brain wandered over the recent happenings in the city. Could all that frenzied activity really be the result of the Old Codger's prophecies? Likewise the events here on Lickey Top? If so, the paths of destiny hardly ran smooth. To the bug's computer-like mind, this destiny business seemed rather a hit-and-miss affair. So what if some interfering busybody tugged a string that wasn't supposed to be pulled? What if some ingenious mind plotted counter to that divine plan? Would not that destiny be thrown awry, and out of gear? But who was there conceited and bold enough to pit himself against such an opponent? The insect knew only one such spirit. Who else but an extremely rare, seven-legged, orange-backed cockle-snorkle? Destiny, he scoffed silently, where was its logic, its carefully laid plans? Oh, what a feather in someone's cap to challenge and defeat it. To make destiny itself dance to one's tune. The giggles of the cockle-snorkle merged with the chuckles of the tossing and turning owl, blending with the self-satisfied grunts of the Old Codger, browsing at the foot of the tree. . . .

9 Dawn Stirrings

'I did exactly as you told me,' hissed the Sneak. 'I stood him in the brightest light I could find.'

'So how did he escape Black Shadow?' spat Zero. The two sat alone against the cellar wall. The rest of the Mob were asleep.

The Sneak shrugged. 'I only obey orders. So luck was with him. How is that my fault?'

'Are you sure it was he?' demanded Zero. 'It was dark, remember. You could have been mistaken.'

'We got back from the raid,' said the Sneak, sighing as he went over it again. 'While the Mob were stacking the loot I heard a noise outside. I poked my head out into the alley-way and feeling suddenly brave, ran down to investigate. I was just in time to see the Decoy plunge into the canal, leaving Black Shadow spitting on the bank. The mouse swam out to that old boat. I heard the Basin Swingers welcoming him aboard, then fear gripped me. I ran back here like a bat out of hell. And that's it.'

Zero's eyes glittered with hate and frustration. He muttered beneath his breath as he tenderly nursed his still swollen tail.

'My, but you've really got it in for that Decoy,' whispered the Sneak with a shiver. 'Is it because he whipped you in a fair fight and made you look foolish? Or is the real reason much deeper and more sinister?

Like because he reminds you of the once threatening Chosen mouse?'

'He broke the oath by deserting,' snapped Zero unconvincingly. 'That is reason enough.'

'But say you really did fear him,' persisted the Sneak. 'So he's hopped it. If my guess is right, wild horses couldn't drag him back here. Wouldn't it be simpler to forget about him? You know, out of sight and out of mind, and all that?'

'It's the ones you forget about who do for you,' was Zero's hoarse reply. Now he was shivering slightly, as if at some secret thought. He continued, the words low and self directed, 'He was a leader in his own land. . . . So long as that mouse lives, we can never feel secure.'

All the malice in his black soul shone out through his close-set eyes, causing the odious Sneak to shrink away. For a while neither spoke. Only the steady breathing of the Mob and the odd burp from one of the bully-mice disturbed that icy silence. Stealing glances at Zero, the Sneak was praying he hadn't said too much. It was so easy to become a marked mouse – just a word out of place was enough. A crawler the Sneak might be, but that was because he wanted desperately to live. For he had a burning ambition. Often and secretly, he had promised himself that one day he would reach the top of the heap, and stay there. And when that glorious day came, the reign of Zero would seem like a Sunday picnic. Suddenly a voice broke into those delicious thoughts. Not Zero's, but an alien one. Instantly on guard, the two mice were sitting up, heads turned towards the entrance to the cellar. For a while they remained frozen and blinking, for the flash of orange light had momentarily blinded them.

'I'll say it again, and for the last time.' The voice was

high-pitched and sharp – obviously one used to getting its own way. 'I am here to save you from your own stupidity. What I have to say will benefit you greatly. Ignore me at your peril.' The mice stared apprehensively. Perched on a brick a foot or two before them was a now very drab insect.

'Why, it's just a creepy-crawly,' scoffed the Sneak. 'Admittedly with an amazing ability to flash bright orange at will, but a creepy-crawly for all that. What were we talking about, Zero?'

'Don't turn your backs on me,' warned the cockle-snorkle. 'For I know things that would make your toes curl.'

'And I have a paw to crush you flat,' retorted Zero. 'I am the leader of the Gas Street Mob and not used to being spoken to like that.'

'He's right,' nodded the Sneak, his yellow streak undulating. 'Zero holds many lives in the palm of his paw. Beware, little orange flea.'

'Power?' said the scornful bug. 'You boast to me of power? I have more power in my spare leg than the whole of your Mob put together.'

'Squash him!' ordered Zero angrily. The Sneak rose to obey. Immediately the bug flew into the air, to alight upon a rafter just above. For a while he stayed there grinning. Then he sped down to perch upon the brick once more.

'When you say power, you mean brute force,' he corrected. 'And quite useless if you can't bring it into play. Herein lies real power.' He tapped his head with a spare leg, his eyes bright with pride. Then he was all scorn again. 'Claws to tear . . . teeth to rip . . . paws to crush . . . even stings to shock . . . what use these things against me? I was blessed with the weapon of weapons – a tongue to lash this stupid world. If I say black is white you'll believe it. If I say day is night start counting stars. In short, I have the gift of the gab and am invincible. . . . '

'So what do you want with us?' asked Zero peevishly. The authority in the bug's voice had truly shaken him. Now he felt vulnerable beneath that direct stare.

'Don't ask me why, but I am of a mind to help you,' said the bug. 'But first let me demonstrate just who you are dealing with. The Chosen mouse, for instance. Very unfortunate his accident, eh? But to give you a real fright, would you like to know his whereabouts?'

'The Chosen mouse is dead,' sneered Zero. 'Black Shadow took him.'

'Correction,' shot back the bug. 'The Chosen mouse is alive and kicking. In fact Fox of Furrowfield took him, but that's by the way.'

'The Chosen mouse alive?' screamed the Sneak. 'Are you trying to tell us he has returned from Heaven knows where, glowing with health and strength? And for revenge, naturally. Will he never forgive Zero for his dastardly deed?'

'Why should I need forgiveness?' asked Zero, his eyes like glowing pools of fire.

'Sorry, slip of the tongue,' the Sneak gabbled. 'Sometimes I put two and two together. I hope I live to regret it.'

'Keep hoping,' snapped Zero. 'And keep your mouth shut too.' He turned a wary eye back to the bug. 'You say the Chosen mouse lives? So tell us another joke.'

'Certainly,' came the cheerful reply. 'How's this for funny? At this very moment he is gathering a great strength in the countryside – in preparation for your overthrow, of course. So laugh.'

'If there was only some way I could stop my knees from knocking,' said the terrified Sneak. 'For I am hanging on to every word of this bug's story. Now I am racking my brains, trying to remember if I ever tried to frame the Chosen mouse. For some reason, folk bear grudges. I am desperately trying to stand my ground, but I'm liable to bolt at any moment. . . .'

'I wouldn't give a fig for your chances,' growled Zero, his tones an echo of doom. But he had also developed a paw-twitch. The bug's story was beginning to get to him, too.

'No falling out now,' chided the cockle-snorkle. 'We must stick together in these troubled times. All is lost when villains fall out.'

Zero struggled to regain control of his shaking limbs. But his voice betrayed him. It echoed shrill and shaky in his ears. 'How do you know all this? Can you prove the Chosen mouse lives?'

'He intends to do that himself,' giggled the bug. 'Sooner or later he and his great strength will come surging in through that hole in the wall. So think on, time is running out for you two.'

Zero's paw-tremble had spread. Even his whiskers were vibrating in horror. All the cowardly instincts in his being surged to the fore. And to make his humiliation complete, the insect was watching him, his eyes filled with contempt. Zero's next words were a bare croak. 'You have actually seen him? You speak of a great strength? Where would he find that in a strange land?'

'From within himself, I believe,' replied the bug mysteriously. 'But now I must add to your miseries. You have another mortal enemy even closer to hand. Down in the Basin, to be precise. I hear on good authority he intends to join forces with the Chosen mouse, when that one returns from the countryside. That's if he doesn't lose patience and try to topple you on his own. He has been heard muttering about being exposed beneath a bright light . . . being left to die, in fact. My, but he's a nasty bit of work when he's roused.'

'Name him,' whimpered Zero, although knowing full well to whom the bug referred.

'None other than the missing Decoy Third Class,' replied the grave-faced bug, lying like there was no tomorrow. 'He has taken on the guise of a busking minstrel. By way of a glorious singing voice, he has wormed his ticket into the Basin Swingers. They are now an ambitious quartet. It's a ploy, of course. His entry into the music scene is a sideline. His real ambition is to make mincemeat of Zero.'

'But why?' Zero's terror was now total. 'What have I done to him?'

'What have you done?' hooted the bug merrily. 'Does the victim love his executioner? On the other hand he may dislike the way your eyes are set too close together. Or the disgusting way you moult fur all over the place. He could have a dozen reasons for despising you. Added all together they spell murder. What's the betting he might try to corner you alone some time?'

'I wish I could corner that Decoy in a friendly way,' sighed the Sneak. 'If he starts toppling folk, he might forget who his best friend is. You may ask why I have hopped up upon the fence? It is because Zero has lost his nerve, and cannot think positively. As a simple mouse, I am badly in need of leadership at this moment in time.'

'So the rats desert the sinking ship,' mused the bug. 'I can't say I'm surprised.'

'Perhaps I could think of a good sideline,' said the

Sneak, thoughtfully stroking his whiskers. 'How's this? Do you think the Basin Swingers could use a willing mouse to keep time with his paw? But it's no good, music always left me cold. So how about this? How about if I went down to the Basin and said –.'

'Set one paw outside that hole and you will be a goner in five seconds flat,' warned Zero. 'You and I are in this together.' He turned to the cockle-snorkle. Now his eyes were softly watering, as he addressed the grinning bug. 'Perhaps you would take my side?' he asked, piteously imploring. 'If you could keep us informed of enemy movement, we could beat off this cowardly twin attack, when it came?'

'I never take sides,' replied the firm bug. 'My style is to play ends against the middle. In this case, three ends. But before the tears start flowing, yes, I will help. But always remember, I am liable to turn against you without warning. Your sordid little scrap is of no interest to me. I battle against the greatest adversary of all – destiny. Suffice it to say, I intend to confound and turn that imposter inside out. . . . '

'Of course, of course,' agreed Zero, hastily. He hadn't a clue what the bug was talking about, but clutching at straws as he was he desperately needed help. It was not a pretty sight: Zero the tyrant near to blubbering. Yet behind that woebegone visage lurked a terrible, blind rage. Zero felt trapped and cornered, and was, in such a mood, doubly dangerous. He spoke, his tone ugly. 'Tell us where along the canal the Decoy is hiding out. We could then creep along the bank, and bash him to pulp.'

'Crude,' replied the bug, shaking his head. 'No wonder your partner has itchy paws. Let me think.' He pretended to be deep in thought. For a while only the steady breathing of the sleeping Mob disturbed the long silence.

'This tension is becoming unbearable,' wept the Sneak. 'I feel myself to be a pawn in someone else's game. I am really keyed up now. I am so frightened I am kidding myself I can reach that hole in the wall in four seconds flat. For mercy's sake stop me, for here I go –.'

'I've got it,' sang the bug, having had it all along. Typically, he had been enjoying baiting the cowardly pair. Thankfully, the Sneak sank down the wall, his legs numb and rubbery. Zero heaved a great sobbing sigh and also relaxed somewhat. 'The plan is this,' said the bug, gleefully rubbing his front legs together. 'We will deal with the Decoy first. As he is the nearer this makes perfect sense. My idea is to lure him into the cellar. Tell me, what would please the Basin Swingers most in this world?'

'To hit the big-time and become famous, of course,' said Zero mystified.

'In short, they yearn for an audience to applaud their caterwauling? In fact, they would give their eye-teeth to be invited here to entertain you?' nodded the bug.

'Who listens to good music these days?' scoffed the Sneak. 'Anyway, we can't stand arty types, they always seem to be enjoying life as though it's just a bowl of cherries.'

'Don't interrupt,' snapped the bug. 'And don't underestimate the power of music. For some strange reason, music makes some folk feel happy and confident. There lies the danger. What we don't want is a minstrel mouse brimming with confidence, swimming back over the canal, pouncing on poor Zero, and thrashing him within an inch of his life. Or worse . . . .'

Zero's nerves snapped. He dashed across to the hole in the wall, and peered out. Such was his panic he almost forgot that Black Shadow might be lurking behind the dustbins, for that one patrolled the city till dawn. But Zero, in his fear, could only imagine the Chosen mouse returning in strength from the countryside; and simultaneously, Pentecost, brimming with confidence, marching up from the canal. For, simple soul, he believed the bug's lies – even wanted to, for Zero's disturbed mind was complex indeed. Often in dreams he saw the whole city rising up against a tyrant. But in his private fancy it was he, Zero, who always led that uprising. For, hating himself as he did, he understood why others should as well.

'Cool minds and steady nerves,' the bug was saying. 'Otherwise we might as well forget it. So do you want to hear my plan?' Shame-faced, Zero returned to slump against the wall.

'You will arrange a concert,' said the brisk bug. 'You will invite the Basin Swingers as star performers. They will accept, of course, for musicians are a vain lot. When they arrive you will seize their contralto. Don't worry about the water-rats, for I know something they haven't thought of. If I said their talents were too large for this flea-pit cellar, you wouldn't understand, so let's skip it. What is important is, you will have enemy number one in your clutches.'

'Why should we seize their contralto?' interrupted the perplexed Sneak. 'Surely the one we want is their bass-singer?'

'Explain,' sighed the bug wearily.

'Because the bass-singer will be the missing Decoy, of course,' was the reply. 'It is the natural order of things. Everyone starts at the bottom in life. Only then can one join the free-for-all climb. The methods vary, of course. For myself I prefer the buttering-up and betrayal technique. . . . '

'What a pathetic mouse you are.' The bug sounded almost sad. 'All this scrabbling and plotting – and for what? How glad I am to be above all that, and with a whole world to bustle in. But come, let us conclude our business. I have other urgent fish to fry. The contralto is the one you want, so no more nonsense.'

'I will recognise his floppy ears anywhere,' muttered Zero vengefully. 'As soon as he sets paw through that hole, I will send in my bully-mice. He'll be sorry he ever broke the oath of the Gas Street Mob.'

'And bit your tail,' reminded the Sneak. 'But remember to keep well out of his way. It's no secret that Decoy could wipe the floor with you anytime.'

His words went unheeded. Zero was frowning. A thought had struck him. 'What if when we invite them, they try to work a trio on us?'

'Just insist upon the quartet or nothing,' said the bug, promptly. 'But there's no problem, for I have been saving my stroke of genius till last. To make sure the Decoy comes you will offer him a full pardon. It must be offered sincerely, of course. With paws on hearts, and with smiles. If he still holds back, the water-rats' lust for fame will swing the balance. He'll come, even if they have to drag him. Just be your natural cunning self, and lie with a smile.'

'Have you ever seen Zero smile?' asked the Sneak with a shudder. 'His grin is as cold as the grave. If I saw Zero approaching with a smile on his face, I would take off like a bat out of hell.'

'So who would smile with my problems?' snarled Zero. 'You can do the smiling. I will hardly be in the mood, anyway. Don't forget, I am the one he intends to overthrow.'

'I will practice my sickly-sweet smile,' promised the Sneak.

'So that's clear, then?' said the satisfied bug. Then, curiously: 'By the way, when do you plan to begin the operation? The sooner the better, I say. What day is this?'

'Friday,' said the Sneak. He glanced out at the pale light. 'Just coming up dawn.'

'Tonight's your night, then,' said the bug. 'Sometime today you will go down to the Basin and arrange the concert. If you can remember your lines, the mouse will be in your power before before the moon rises. . . .' His words trailed away. The Sneak was looking at him incredulously. Zero was shuffling his paws, and staring at the ground. 'Now what?' enquired the impatient insect.

'A concert on Friday night?' said the Sneak, open-mouthed with shock. 'Are you quite mad?' Zero glumly nodded in agreement.

'So what's wrong with that?' The bug was looking from one to the other in puzzlement.

'Saturday night is concert night,' reproved the Sneak. 'In the old days, concerts were always held on a Saturday night. That was before Zero put the block on them for his own spiteful reasons. Who ever heard of a wing-ding on Friday night? Where have you been all your life?'

'Out in the great big changing modern world,' retorted the angry bug. 'You think I'm mad? So what does that make you? At any moment the enemy might come charging through that hole, and yet you fuss over trivialities? Are you going to let some bygone ritual rob you of victory? What are you, decadent or something?'

'You can call us what you wish,' said the indignant Sneak. 'But tradition is tradition. It's Saturday night or nothing.'

The bug knew he was on a loser. It was no use. He would not change the minds of the two mice who sat in stubborn silence, their snouts firmly set. If they were afraid of meeting his angry glare, they need not have worried. Although for a while astonished and angered, the cockle-snorkle was now enjoying the funny side. Their sullen stupidity had brought a wide smile to that bright little face. Despite this set-back he had done what he intended. Zero and the Sneak had fallen in with his plan. So what would a day matter? It could even be of help. There was lots to do, and thinking about it, the bug could use the extra time. There was the Pentecost mouse to visit. And what of Fox and the Chosen one? Had they set out for the city? Could they be half-way here already? And then there was the family back home on Lickey Top to be kept on its toes. And Owl. Indeed, the busy insect had plenty to do. So much so, he suddenly felt impatience rising within him. He left as quickly as he had arrived, and without a goodbye.

Left alone, the devious pair quietly discussed the coming Saturday night. There was a problem. It was the Sneak who raised it.

'I am worrying about the more honourable members of the Mob,' he whispered. 'Do you think some of them will object to the plan? They will agree that the missing Decoy should die for breaking the oath . . . but might not some of them think the method to capture him sneaky? Will they say to offer a full pardon, only to withdraw it, is not playing the game? I'm thinking of the Scout First Class in particular. He could cause problems.'

'That's another mouse who's heading for the chop,' spat Zero. 'I'm only waiting for the right moment. As for the rest of them, we will simply say we have arranged the concert to brighten up their lives. We will casually mention that in order to do this, we offered the Decoy a full pardon. If anyone comes the honourable bit and objects we will just have to smooth them over. The important thing is to get that dangerous mouse in our clutches. Then, once inside this cellar he will meet with an unfortunate accident. Only when he is out of the way can we turn our attention to the Chosen mouse. But remember, not a word to anyone that those two mice plan to join forces to overthrow me.'

'That would be foolhardy,' said the Sneak. 'If the Mob learned that, they would probably go over to their side en masse. I suspect that is what many are waiting for – some mouse to bravely attempt your downfall.'

Zero twiddled his paws nervously, but remained silent.

'Just imagine what would happen if the Mob found out those avenging mice wanted only your skin?' pressed the Sneak. 'Not that I'd tell them. Which brings me to another question I am burning to ask. Am I certain to rise in the world quite soon? I hope that doesn't sound like blackmail, Zero? But should a high and safe post fall vacant, would I be the first in line for it? Only, if I remain at the bottom of the heap much longer, I will go spare with worry. I am sometimes tempted to run out of the hole in the wall in under five seconds, and throw in my lot with the returning Chosen mouse. . . .'

'I am planning something special for you when this is all over,' said Zero, raising his eyes heavenwards. 'You will be rewarded, never fear.'

'Now I feel really confident and happy,' sighed the

Sneak. 'I love being your partner in this power-struggle. I love even more being the junior partner. For then if something should go wrong, it's your head on the block. Thank you for trusting me, Zero. Can I call you my best friend? It will make me so glad, for I have been so unlucky with my friends. The Scout proved to be untrue. . . . The Decoy ran out on me. . . . I hope you won't hurt me like that, Zero?'

'As if I would,' said the other softly. He was staring into space and only half listening.

'May I take a liberty and put a paw around you?' whispered the Sneak. And he did. It was a sight to chill the blood, those two, expressing an affection they could feel for no-one. It was a sight the Scout First Class shuddered at. His ears had been affronted, too. For he had heard every word that had passed between the bug and that plotting pair. Now he lay tussling with his loyalties, and his conscience. . . .

10 A Concert is Arranged

It was breakfast time down in the Basin. For a mouse called Pentecost it was a miserable one indeed. Hungry as he was, the smell from the offered fish turned his stomach. Thanking the water-rats for their kind thought, he rose, paws slipping on the slush of stagnant water and fish-scales that slicked the deck of the narrow-boat. Listlessly, he explored, pausing to nibble at the greasy moss that grew between the warped planks of the old craft. To his surprise, it tasted better than it looked. As the hunger-pangs subsided, so Pentecost realised with a start that this was the first time he had eaten since leaving the Gas Street cellar. The food set him thinking of home. The family on Lickey Top would be enjoying their breakfast about now. Sweet-roots, an ear of wheat, and perhaps as a treat, the blackberries would be ripe? Then self-pity overcame him. Valiantly he strove against that gnawing feeling, and tried to think of other things. But he could see only danger and heart-ache everywhere he cast his mind. For kind as they appeared, the water-rats, though they would not admit to it, held him prisoner, albeit ever so gently. Turning, Pentecost saw the right side-kick watching him carefully, a smile playing about his face. . . .

Breakfast over, Zero and the Sneak excused themselves. They were, they said, going to suss out a possible cheese source. Their explanation was accepted by the Mob. Only the Scout knew what they were really up to. But he said nothing. A stodgy though honourable mouse, he was thinking things through in his long-winded way. Doubtless he would arrive at a solution to his dilemma, but, typically, he would go all around the houses to reach it. His problem was an awesome one for a mouse of his sensibilities. Outwardly cold-hearted, he would ponder long and hard. Inwardly warm-hearted, he would cogitate deeply. Where in this impossible situation lay his loyalties? Should he side with evil and thus help hurry the fled Decoy to his death, or should he denounce what he knew was a terrible wrong? He just did not know. So he thought on and said nothing. . . .

'Ahoy the Basin Swingers!' yelled Zero from the shore. 'A humble Gas Street mouse requests the pleasure of a concert in our lowly home, if your time and talent will allow. But if you are fully booked up, we will understand.' His shoulders slumped as he turned to trudge dejectedly away. From the side of his mouth he hissed for the Sneak to do likewise. It was a fine bit of tragic acting from the pair.

'Stop!' cried the surprised right side-kick. 'It so happens we have a cancelled performance. Only one, mind. Apart from that our gigs are a lock-out.'

'We were banking on Saturday night,' called Zero, turning back. Respectfully he added, 'But perhaps you are too exclusive to perform in front of huge, jostling audiences? If you consent, I promise our Mob will keep as quiet as mice. . . . But no, they love to clap and cheer so much, you see. We apologise for wasting your time.' Again he turned to make a miserable departure. The Sneak, a quick catcher-on, beat him to it this time.

'Wait!' yelled the frantic left side-kick. 'Providing the applause comes at the end of each song we will accept the engagement.'

'Do you speak for the quartet or merely the trio?' asked Zero quickly. 'Only we have our hearts set on hearing the new blending tenor.'

'Would you settle for something a mite higher?' asked King, his mellow voice trembling with excitement. 'For our tenor contralto has no limit to his range. Each passing hour seems to increase his tense pitch. No screaming, you understand, for he is in perfect control.'

Zero pretended to be taken aback. In an awed voice, he said, 'To hear a rich tenor we merely hoped for. But to be honoured by a shrill contralto exceeds our wildest dreams. We can expect you Saturday night?'

'Never!' shouted Pentecost, defiantly. 'For I am under pain of death for breaking the oath, though I didn't,

148

really. I haven't betrayed you to a rival Mob. I just decided to become a singer instead.'

'Let's hope your voice doesn't break,' shouted the Sneak, his voice filled with a joyous hope. 'For you have reached the top of the tree, warbling-wise. And always remember, quartets have a habit of splitting up. Where would you go then? But you could always come running to me, your best friend. A mouse on his way down can always bank on my sympathy –'. Zero cut him short with a vicious nudge.

'You stood me in a bright light!' cried Pentecost angrily. 'What kind of friend would do that?'

'That's Show Business,' the Sneak retorted, ignoring Zero's hissed asides. 'In fact, come Saturday night, I intend to stand you in an even brighter one. Believe me, I am following your career with the greatest interest.'

'You were hoping Black Shadow would get me,' continued Pentecost accusingly. 'Now you are trying to lure me back into the Gas Street cellar. I know Zero plans to kill me. The concert is just a trick. Well, you don't fool me, nor my friends.'

'Come now,' murmured the left side-kick. 'Don't let's be too harsh. I am sure these music-loving mice are truly sorry, and wish only to make amends.'

'And so we do,' called Zero promptly. 'For we have yet to mention the full pardon. You have been granted one. At my urging, the whole Mob agreed upon it.' Despite the gloom, the smile of the Sneak was bright and sickly-sweet. Practised and honed, it was sliced melon wide, and honey-dripping. 'As of now your slate is wiped clean and all is forgiven,' assured Zero. 'And, frankly, I now realise you weren't cut out to be a Decoy. The world is in much greater need of good singers.'

'But if you are still in doubt, I will put your mind at rest,' said the Sneak, his smile a friendly quirk now. 'Only this morning we took a vote on who was the most popular deserter, ever. Guess who won, paws down?'

Smoothly, Zero added, 'So you see, you have nothing to fear from us. Now, the concert. Will Saturday night suit your time-table? Just before sunset? As your know, Black Shadow comes on point-duty at the first hint of creepy darkness. . . .'

'I think we can manage that,' said the right side-kick grandly. 'In the meantime, we will rehearse like mad. The world has yet to hear our new blues medley.'

'And when they hear our King . . . ' exclaimed his jubilant partner, ' . . . for this could be the start of something big . . . .'

'Like a star is born,' sighed the wistful Sneak. 'I wish I'd got rhythm. . . . '

Mission accomplished, a satisfied Zero called across the water for the last time. 'We will expect you Saturday night just before sunset, then? The Mob will be over the moon when we tell them. We will hurry home and organise refreshments and things.' With that he scampered off up the alley, the Sneak in hot pursuit.

So great was the joy of the water-rats, none of them saw the fear and concern on Pentecost's face. In truth, they didn't want to. The trio hugged each other, whooping their happiness as they pranced about the deck of the boat. It was King who finally noticed something was amiss. Sober now, he said, 'My ears tell me our country friend does not share our good fortune? We realise he misses his home, but surely he is a little pleased the way his new career has taken off so suddenly?'

'I'm happy for the trio, I truly am,' said the unhappy mouse. 'But for the quartet, I see only peril ahead. You must know the concert is a trap? Please believe me, I wish you all the fame in the world; but for myself I would rather take my chances, and attempt to escape from the city.'

The water-rats were suddenly downcast. They were sharing similar thoughts. Just when success chose to smile on them, so the group seemed set to break up. The pattern was a familiar one in the entertainment business. The reproach in those pairs of eyes, and the sad lowering of King's head, moved the mouse. He knew how much the concert meant to them. But he also knew what it would mean for him if he ever set foot in the Gas Street cellar. Only now was he beginning to learn how naïve and innocent musicians could be. He spoke, but gently.

'Surely you could become a trio again? You sang beautifully before I came along with my top C, which was never all it should be.'

'But they insist upon a quartet,' said the broken-voiced left side-kick.

Pentecost was desperate now. 'But is an audience so very important? Isn't making music for your own ears satisfying enough?'

The right side-kick, so kindly up till now, was no longer smiling. His face was set and determined. There was a harsh edge to his voice as he spoke. 'Didn't we take you in when you had nowhere to go? Didn't we offer you a place in our group? And didn't you accept? Now you would break your contract. You wish to run out on us just when our big chance arrives.'

'Ungrateful, selfish mouse,' scowled his partner.

'False friend!' boomed King, his sightless eyes brimming with tears.

'Thank heaven the mouse is only joking and doesn't mean it,' said the right side-kick, smiling again. 'He is simply suffering from first night nerves.'

'As if he would really let us down,' said the second small water-rat, warmth creeping back into his tone. 'If we keep him close beside us, all his fears will melt away. We will take turns to watch over him until Saturday night. All he needs is companionship, and lots of hugging.'

King suddenly reached out, his paws fumbling. Pentecost felt himself enveloped by a gentle but extremely firm limb. He was under no illusions now. He was a prisoner, and though treated with respect and courtesy, trapped in the kindliest of gaols.

'Let us sing of silver linings!' cried the right side-kick. 'For every cloud has one, God bless us.'

'Amen,' boomed King, his senses tingling like quicksilver. He crushed close the unresisting mouse.

At last Pentecost's worst fears were realised. As the water-rats began to sing, so all hope left him. Since leaving Lickey Top he had learned many harsh lessons. Here was another. A foe was not always one who bore his enmity bold before him. A foe could appear in the friendliest of guises. For the water-rats would do him down as surely as Zero and the Sneak, who, had they remained to witness this scene, would have rubbed their paws in glee. For who more than they knew the lure of ambition? But the singing trio knew not, and cared less what they did. Pentecost had been embraced by his most relentless enemies to date, their menace a love of music, and the foolish belief that the most savage heart could be soothed by it. With a smile and a hopeful glance at the stars, they would lead Pentecost, late of Lickey Top, to his death in the Gas Street cellar on

Saturday night. For they saw through the quartet a means to a place amongst those twinkling points of light. No matter that the night of the concert would be dark and cloudy, and the silver linings they sang about existed only in the minds of fools. . . .

There was a death in the Gas Street alley that morning. As Zero and the Sneak pattered homeward, so a mouse on an errand of mercy hurried down towards the Basin. Hugging the wall for the shadow there, he had no wish to be detected. But he was. For as he stole along he muttered to himself. It was this the evil pair heard. Zero hissed a command and he and his companion froze, their ears alert, as they listened to the soul-searching traitor. Now his words were plainly heard. He seemed to be rehearsing a speech as he scurried past.

'I warn you in the spirit of friendship,' the mouse was saying. 'And though I have always avoided close contact with others, I feel a warmth I cannot contain. For I realise I regard you with affection, despite my cold nature. As you saved my life, so I will try to preserve yours. I do this with a free and open heart, and yes, in true friendship. So I say beware . . . . Beware the Saturday night concert –.'

The rest of his words were choked off as Zero and the Sneak pounced. There was a cry, a scuffle, then silence. Moments later a small and limp form was stuffed behind a stinking dustbin. Soon the nimble killers were hurtling for the hole in the wall. They vanished inside. . . .

There was a death in the alley that morning. Destiny decreed there would be so. But the soul of the victim was soon to journey to a better place. To a far better place, for the Scout First Class had died with honour.

If Pentecost believed he had hit rock bottom, he was wrong. Great though his despair, he was to suffer more. But first his hopes would be raised.

'Tell me,' said the right side-kick, pausing in mid-song and nudging the others, 'what would an extra voice make us?'

'You're right,' agreed his partner. 'We have been a quintet for the last two choruses.'

'I thought we sounded off key,' remarked King, his sensitive ears quivering.

'Hello,' called the right side-kick. 'Is there anybody there?'

'Three guesses,' came a cheerful voice. 'So what do you think? Did I pass the audition?'

'Cockle-snorkle!' cried Pentecost, his eyes shining with hope as the bug winged down from the roof of the tunnel. 'I never thought I'd be glad to hear your voice. I'm in the most terrible trouble.'

'You ain't kidding,' remarked the bug, perching on a coil of rope on top of the cabin. 'It's certainly gone sour, this mission of yours. Remember how you set off, all eager and confident? Never mind, I've got this destiny business well in hand. Each time it deals you a savage blow, I shall give it one back. We'll see who's the master yet. Mind you, there will be more hardships and heart-breaks before I sort it all out, but then you must be used to those by now.'

'I've experienced nothing else,' blurted the mouse in anguish. 'My only hope is for Fox to return and rescue me. Would you know if he's set out yet?'

'Are you keeping count of these savage blows?' warned the bug. 'For here's another. It appears Fox has got himself a new pal. You do remember the Chosen mouse?'

'But he's dead!' cried Pentecost, astonished. 'Black Shadow took him.'

'Then what's he doing rolling in daisies and clover?' asked the bug. 'He and Fox are inseparable these days. Strolling about Furrowfields, laughing, and discussing the meaning of life . . . it's quite touching to see.'

'The Chosen mouse is in the Lickey Hills?' gasped Pentecost. 'My double escaped Black Shadow? And he has taken my place in Fox's affections? I can't believe it. He's such a sharp-tongued, irritating mouse.' He stopped short, realising he could have been describing himself in his former, selfish days.

'Steel yourself,' said the bug, hiding his delight. 'Fox told me the whole story, and it isn't pretty from your point of view. It seems when you vanished into the cellar Fox hung around for a while. Then when the Chosen mouse came hurtling out, Fox decided to cut his losses. He thought . . . well, a mouse is a mouse for all that, and he does look like the Pentecost pest. So he took him back to Lickey Top. Then something happened. True love came creeping. Fox and the Chosen mouse shyly discovered a rapport. In Fox's own words . . . "This Chosen mouse is the friend I've been waiting for all my life."'

'But surely he spared a thought for me, trapped in the cellar?' cried Pentecost, his head in a whirl. 'Didn't Fox even consider poking a questing paw into the cellar, in the hope of making contact? But why should he abandon me in favour of the Chosen mouse? I know I sometimes taxed his patience, but deep down I knew he never held it against me.'

'Perhaps you finally taxed him too far,' shrugged the bug. 'For faced with the choice of rescuing you or carrying the Chosen mouse to safety, he chose the latter course. Only yesterday I took him to task about it. "Fox," I said sternly, "what about the Pentecost mouse, lost in the city? Is this the way to treat a pal?"'

'And what did he reply?' asked Pentecost anxiously. 'Did he appear to be filled with remorse?'

The bug shook his head gloomily. 'Fox replied, very stiffly, and pointing to the Chosen mouse, "This is my only pal." Then he patted his new friend with a fond paw. It was so upsetting I had to turn my head away.'

'What does the family think of it all?' cried a bewildered Pentecost. 'Were they very angry when they learned Fox had run out on me?'

'I'm afraid the savage blows are coming thick and fast this morning,' sighed the bug. 'But don't fret, I am working on Uncle Pentecost. I am trying to get him to change his stubborn mind. It won't be easy, though, for he has put his sore paw down very gently, in order to be firm. He has outlawed you, and I'm afraid the family are behind him all the way. They swear if you ever poke you nose out of the Weasel Woods again . . . but I can't go on, it's all too distressing. . . .'

'Uncle Pentecost?' echoed the dazed mouse. 'You did say Uncle Pentecost? Am I going quite mad? Surely the family wouldn't promote him in my place? Didn't you or Fox explain to them that it was destiny, as foretold by the Old Codger, that led me to the city? Surely they haven't branded me a frivolous mouse, and washed their paws of me?'

The bug attempted to look woebegone, and succeeded. 'Upon the strict orders of Uncle Pentecost, the little ones are now chanting, "What deserting leader, we cannot recall who you mean?" I'm afraid you are fast becoming a dim memory back home on Lickey Top.'

Never was a mouse more totally broken in heart and

spirit. The world of Pentecost had finally crashed about his floppy ears. He buried his snout in his paws, and shook with sobs.

'The red poet has forsaken his blue friend,' King's deep voice broke into the grief-laden air. 'But perhaps it was meant to be. I believe that destiny sent this mouse to us. And though he has lost much, yet he will gain in other ways. His compensation for losing everything he holds dear will be fame. Once we were a struggling group; now, because of this mouse, we have been invited to entertain the Gas Street Mob in their cellar. Destiny has brought this about.'

'And this little insect must be destiny's messenger,' remarked the right side-kick. 'Who – for the benefit of King – is orange, gauzily-winged, and comically-legged.'

'A lopsided horse-fly, in fact,' said the left side-kick promptly. 'With a lot of say for himself, and a strangely mean look about the eyes.'

'Horse-fly nothing,' retorted the bug. 'And neither am I anyone's messenger. You say destiny arranged this concert? Well, I say I did. Destiny indeed! I mean to turn it topsy-turvy. I am already one jump ahead. So who asked for the opinions of a bunch of beat-up blues balladeers?'

'This little slave of fate certainly has a gift for wordy lies,' said the right side-kick scathingly. 'Even though he can't carry a tune. But then the gift of words and music seldom come in one package. He is probably one of those types who like to hang around up-and-coming groups, eager to jump on their bandwagon.'

'If he seeks to join us he will be unlucky,' said his partner. 'I think we can dismiss him as a humble go-between 'twixt us and destiny, but with delusions of grandeur.'

'Join you?' scoffed the bug. 'It was I who set your bandwagon rolling. I could just as easily bring it to a grinding halt. As the most skilful double agent on earth, there is nothing I can't do.'

'You, an agent?' said the right side-kick, suddenly interested. 'Now an agent we can use. Though you would need to tone down your enthusiasm, for many a group has come unstuck through being double-booked.'

'He could spread the word, and get us more widely known,' said his friend, excited at the prospect.' And with his gift for exaggeration, I'll bet he could dream up some smashing slogans.'

'Like . . . "The Second City Swingers Sing Soul",' shouted the right side-kick. 'That would be one in the eye for those sneerers in the south, don't you think?'

'Cockle-snorkle,' interrupted Pentecost urgently. 'If it's true you arranged this concert, you could equally easily cancel it?'

'A dedicated agent never admits defeat,' replied the bug grandly. 'So what do you wish to beg of me?'

'I know you like to treat everything as a joke,' said the desperate mouse. 'But please, just this once, take into consideration the peril I'm in. Perhaps you thought you were doing us a favour when you arranged the concert. But if you study my case you will see that the booking is a death sentence for me. I beg you, act as our compassionate agent, and persuade the Basin Swingers that the concert would not be in our interest.'

'So,' grinned the bug. 'What happened to our faith in destiny? Beginning to realise only I can save you now?'

'In the absence of Fox, yes,' said Pentecost humbly. 'The prophecy of the Old Codger was all lies, I see this now. My heroic mission has turned out to be one long struggle to stay alive. So I implore you, Cockle-snorkle, please help me. I will do anything you say.'

'I will think about it,' replied the callous insect. 'Mind you, I have an awful lot to do these days. It's all go, you know. However, I will try to fit your problem into my busy schedule.'

The water-rats were listening, and frowning. 'A concert arranged by destiny cannot be cancelled,' butted in the right side-kick. He pulled a protesting Pentecost close, and addressed the grinning bug. 'We have decided to manage without an agent, thank you very much. Now if you will excuse us –.'

'Help me, Cockle-snorkle!' cried Pentecost as he was led firmly away behind the cabin-top. 'And if you see Fox, tell him –.' The rest of his words were quickly stifled. There began a melodious humming, not unlike the sound of twin tuning-forks, as the Basin Swingers launched into a rehearsing session. The song they sang was an especially mournful one, all about stormy weather.

The bug's laughter echoed around the Basin as he darted off across the canal, his bright reflection startling the dreamy water-boatmen and sending them skating for cover. Outside and above the city, storm-clouds were indeed gathering. Soon the insect was dodging the first plump and heavy drops. Then the heavens opened, the torrent hammering on roof-tops, beating at a million window-panes, gurgling down the drains to raise the level of the canal and rocking the boats at their moorings.

As the bug tumbled and rolled amongst the rain-drops, he considered his next move. But first he summed up the events so far. Back home on Lickey Top, law and order was breaking down nicely, and what with

Owl on his back and out of it, complete chaos threatened that place. And here in the city? Now here was more exciting stuff. The Pentecost mouse would soon be attending a concert he would give his life to get out of. The way things were going he might get his wish. The bug proudly congratulated himself that he had arranged that. But his only worry was Fox and the Chosen mouse. Where were they? If they arrived too late in the city, that would certainly spoil things. For the bug did not wish for Pentecost to die. Just to *nearly* die, was his plan for him. For no-one could accuse the cocklesnorkle of thinking cruel thoughts. At least, not too cruel. What he wanted was a dramatic last-ditch rescue attempt, with everyone dashing every which way. The bug was banking on lots of weeping and wailing and beating of breasts, for it pleased his cold little heart to witness distress. But there was something else. The bug was well aware that destiny was busily weaving each and every move. So what a boast to be able to say that one had taken on fate itself, and even though unable quite to beat it, had given it a hell of a run for its money? Suddenly his eyes lit upon the grassy hill that overlooked the city. Now wasn't that a heart-tugging sight? Delightedly, he gazed down. There, streaming with rain, was a 'large red shape', and beside its out-thrust paw, a sodden full-stop that was the Chosen mouse. Lonely they may have looked, but they were not alone. For the same destiny which haunted the singing Basin and the Gas Street cellar, swirled also about that storm-beaten hill. But more intriguing for the bug, it lurked upon a roof-top away over the city, where curled in sleep was the one he had yet to fit into this puzzle. . . .

11 *The Sacrifice*

By late afternoon the rain had ceased. A dull mantle of unbroken cloud lay over the city. Banks of mist obscured all but the tallest buildings and spires. Only the steady hum of traffic gave hint that life still bustled through those thoroughfares. The squatters on the hill exchanged a few final words. A moment later the Chosen mouse was slipping and sliding down the hill, quickly vanishing into the thick, soaking grasses. Some time later he emerged from the foliage at the bottom of the slope to stand shivering on the kerb of the wide black road. He hesitated only briefly. Hastily dashing across, he entered the city and hurried towards his destination, the mists and shadows hiding him from all prying eyes. Reaching a familiar alley-way, he stole into a pile of rotting potato-peelings and craned his ears to hear what was being said inside. . . .

It was a subdued band of mice who gathered for tea in the Gas Street cellar. The news that the Scout First Class had disappeared was sad indeed. Zero's suggestion that the Scout had popped out for a breath of air, only to be surprised by Black Shadow, cut little ice with the more sceptical. They could have reminded the others that the Scout had been a tracker of genius, and that Black Shadow never ventured into the city during the daylight hours. But they didn't. For even if Zero was lying there was no evidence to prove it. Then came another shock.

Zero announced the Sneak's promotion to the missing one's post. This prompted some mutterings about favouritism, and even darker opinions. The one-eyed mouse, always braver than the rest, put a direct question to Zero. Had the leader's supposed trip to suss-out the cheese source, proved successful, and why had neither Zero nor the Sneak reported on such an important subject? Without waiting for a reply he asked another question. And how come the pair just happened to be returning home at about the time the Scout strangely vanished? Wouldn't they have been in the position to witness the event? He seemed ready to ask more probing questions, but Zero hurriedly interrupted him to change the subject. 'We are all deeply saddened to lose the Scout,' he said. 'Indeed, no-one more than myself. If I could bring him back . . . .'

'For he was another trier,' anticipated the Sneak. 'Like the poor Chosen mouse, eh, Zero? You *were* going to say that?'

'I was,' snapped Zero. 'But as you've beaten me to it, I will now tell everyone about the concert, tomorrow night.'

'Concert!' yelled more than one mouse. Suddenly they were all agog. There began much high-spirited jostling amongst the younger mice, for they could sense carnival in the air. The ancients who had served their time as Mob members, and now looked forward only to the Home for Old Mice, or death, seemed especially jovial. They could remember well the concerts of the old days, when a good time was had by all, almost every Saturday night. Relaxing upon their creaking haunches, they smiled cracked smiles, and sat back to listen to the first good news in many a long day. All around, cheers were going up, ringing the rafters and raising a cloud of choking coal-dust. Only the one-eyed mouse and a couple of friends remained wary. It was just like Zero to announce something pleasant, only to cancel it out of spite. But for an old mouse who counted and forgot totals, the news was sweet indeed. Since he had been overthrown by his own son, old Zero had spent many a sleepless night. For try as he might, he had never been able to like his son. In truth, he hated him and yearned for his downfall as eagerly as the next mouse. To have bred such a monster had caused him much pain and puzzlement. But now he felt suddenly light of heart. Could it be his tyrant son was changing for the better? He could certainly hope. He rose to his paws, teeth bared in a yellow grin.

'I hope you realise my old voice is rusty, son?' he joked. Then seriously, 'But I know you will allow us old ones to brush up on tunes and words? It has been a long time since we sang together, you'll understand, son. I can only say this astonishing change in you warms the cockles of my old heart.'

'Sit down, old mouse,' snarled Zero. 'Who wants to listen to your croaking? It so happens I am bringing in outside talent. I have booked the Basin Swingers Quartet to entertain us with mournful blues tomorrow night.'

'Zero means the Basin Swingers Trio,' corrected the one-eyed Second Class Breaker.

'Quartet,' repeated the leader, glaring. 'For it has come to my ears the missing Decoy has joined up with them.'

'Well, it's news to me,' retorted the shamed Breaker, the tips of his ears burning.

There came shocked murmurings from the Mob. Were their ears deceiving them? A condemned Decoy

164

was actually being invited into the cellar as if nothing had happened? It surely could not be. Again Zero's father rose. If he could not sing for the family he could protest on their behalf. Indignantly he said, 'Since when have our laws been turned topsy-turvy? Do you really expect us to applaud a mouse under sentence of death? Well, I won't, for one.'

'Not even if he's genuinely talented?' asked the Sneak reasonably. 'Wouldn't you feel hurt if he refused to cheer the row you make?'

'But I am not under sentence of death!' yelled the bewildered old mouse.

'Neither is the Decoy,' returned the Sneak quickly. 'Zero has granted him a full pardon, with no strings attached.'

The old mouse stayed stubbornly on his feet. 'If I hadn't heard that with my own ears . . .' he said, sadly shaking his head. 'Such a thing would have been unthinkable in my day. These are grave times indeed.'

'"Grave" is not a word I'd bandy about,' muttered the Sneak. 'I think you've said too much already, old mouse. Consider your health.'

'I will be heard!' came the shout. 'I will speak my mind, come hell or high water.'

'What, and miss the concert?' said the Sneak, scuttling over to drape a paw around a fuming old Zero. 'For I'm thinking, one more bleat out of you and your paws won't touch the ground out of that hole. Don't rely on blood being thicker than water where your· son's concerned.'

But the old mouse was not to be deterred by threats at this late stage in his life. If his son chose to throw him from the cellar for speaking his mind, so be it. But they would never get him anywhere near the Queensway

Home for Old Mice. Not on their nelly, they wouldn't. So, bravely, he drew himself up. Before he left this world he was determined to set an example for the impressionable young. Quietly, he spoke.

'Can anyone deny that the Decoy was justly condemned for deserting the Mob? Yet now we learn he is to be pardoned because of a gift for singing. In other words, my toe-rag of a son rates a sing-song above the law. But is that the real reason for this bestowal of mercy? Or are there darker motives lurking inside his black soul? Never forget, little ones, though your bellies rumble with hunger, your heads must always be filled with honour. For I have a feeling in my old bones of trickery afoot. Could it be our just law is being twisted to satisfy a personal hatred? For we all saw that Decoy give my son the thrashing of his life. Is that mouse being lured here by certain criminals I need not name? Shame. If the oath-breaking Decoy must be brought to justice, why not organise a fair, good old-fashioned mouse-hunt, as in my day? For what mockery is this that we condemn, then pardon, only to condemn again, but in the mean spirit of secrecy?'

'Your old dad is really tired of life, isn't he?' observed the Sneak to a scowling Zero. 'And he hasn't finished yet, for he is drawing breath again. . . .'

'There is also the question of the Scout,' thundered the old mouse. 'What really happened to him, I'd like to know?'

'And me,' shouted the one-eyed mouse. 'And a few more others, I'll bet!'

'My paws are clean,' said the Sneak quickly. He edged away from Zero, just in case.

'Traitor,' hissed Zero. He lunged at the Sneak, who nimbly skipped further away still. Instantly the bully-

mice were on their feet, punching their paws and looking for something to attack. At least that was the
impression they gave. In fact they were no use at all. Their
pin-head brains seethed with a lack of understand
ing. Zero, by the nervous look on his face, had just
realised this. He slumped down the wall, his eyes those of a
cornered beast, as his father continued to harangue him.

'I know that mouse well,' old Zero boomed, pointing
a shaking paw. 'Didn't I bring him into the world? How
I wish I had had the courage to see him out of it in those
early days. For sadly, I recognised early what he was
capable of. I am not at all surprised that he plans to
pounce upon a pardoned mouse, while that one is in full
song. I have been aware for a long time that Zero had me
slated for the Queensway Home for Old Mice now my
usefulness is at an end. Well, I will not give him the
pleasure. Instead I will seek a warrior's death in the
claws of Black Shadow. But before I go, I warn you all.
While my wicked son rules the Mob, democracy will
remain forever crushed. My hope is that one day a true
leader will surface. A mouse with courage enough to
sweep away Zero and his rotten hangers-on. And now I
bid you all farewell for ever. . . .'

'Would you like me to count you out?' asked the
unpitying Sneak, helping the old mouse to his shaky
paws and assisting him across to the hole in the wall.
'Though as for counting you back in . . . .'

'I will shift for myself,' came the noble reply. The
one-time Zero the Stubborn shrugged away the repulsive
clutch of the Sneak. Then were heard his departing
words: 'Ponder hard and long, you little ones. I only
hope that my sacrifice will not be in vain.' And then he
was gone into the chill evening air.

After a moment the one-eyed mouse spoke. His words were thoughtful and hinting. 'First the Scout dies, now Zero's old father. Both were mice of honour. Does the Mob think it not strange that death seeks out only good mice? I too pride myself that I know right from wrong. Could it be that I also have little time left to live? And what of the Decoy who has been tricked into coming back here? Many of us saw the way he defended the dead Scout, at the risk of his own life. In my opinion, such a mouse would be incapable of breaking a solemn oath. Yet is he being lured back here in an under-handed way to face that charge? For it is obvious that the concert arranged by Zero is but a cover for that. I demand that Zero comes clean. On behalf of the Gas Street Mob, I demand to know exactly what is going on on, for there is more to all this than meets the eye. What is being withheld from us, that is what I wish to know?'

Even before he had finished, Zero and his bully-mice were bunching together as if for protection against a wrath to come. Had the one-eyed mouse pushed his advantage he could have overthrown Zero there and then. Had he stayed on his feet and given the signal the Mob would have rallied eagerly behind him. But instead, sadly, he promptly sat down for the qualities of leadership were not in him. Bitterly disappointed, the mice began to argue amongst themselves. Zero, hardly able to believe his luck, scrambled to his feet and launched into a rambling speech about loyalty and the importance of standing together, and other such rubbish. The torn family heard him out in silence. But his words held little for them now. They had heard it all before. There was contempt on many faces as he spoke on. The dull-minded bullies apart, there were few souls in that cellar who did not view Zero as the most detestable mouse ever. But a revolt there would not be. For Zero this was relief enough. He was so pleased to be still in one piece he had quite forgotten the purpose of the meeting.

It was the mouse who despised him most of all who set him back on the right track. The Sneak it was who rose to set the blood of the Mob once again racing with anger. For his cunning told him it was time to make the move that, hopefully, would place him in the seat of power tomorrow night. Once he had believed – and shrank from the thought – that only the ousting of Zero could thrust an ambitious mouse to the pinnacle of power. Now if the Mob could be scared into standing full-square behind Zero, the result would be a bloody battle when the Chosen mouse arrived with his strength. And after the two contestants had destroyed each other, a clever mouse, safely perched on the fence, need only slip down to gather up the pieces. Then, slowly and carefully, a mouse with real ambition could build up an army of obedient robots, ready upon a word to hurl themselves upon other Mobs; until, in time, one mouse alone would rule the whole city. The most dangerous mouse alive began to speak. But he was cautious to speak in tones that suggested complete loyalty and concern for his Mob and leader.

'I cannot remain silent any longer!' he cried. 'The leader you silently mock and hate is modestly holding something back. The one-eyed mouse is correct – Zero is indeed withholding something from you. For a grave situation has arisen. In order to prevent panic, our leader decided to keep certain terrible facts to himself. Have you asked yourselves why he watched his beloved father step out to his death? My friends, it is time you heard the truth.'

Zero, recognising the thrown life-line, waved a weakly protesting paw. The Sneak, now in full flow, waved it away in an affectionate but stern manner. 'No, my leader,' he said, shaking his head. 'Your character has been smeared enough. The Mob will hear the truth and then they can judge. It is this: You all remember the idle Chosen mouse who fell to the paw of Black Shadow? Well, he didn't. Somehow he escaped into the countryside –.'

'In fact, quite near the Bull Ring,' murmured a dull-eyed Zero. 'Lickle Tip, I know the place well.'

'Indeed,' said the Sneak, his eyes flashing. 'And there, amidst the rotten fruit the Chosen mouse is sneaking about, raising a great strength. His vow is to return and destroy the family, root and branch. When Zero and I said we were going to suss out a cheese source, we were really on our way to Lickle Tip. We heard and saw the Chosen mouse and his followers. We heard the angry claim that the Gas Street Mob had deliberately thrown the Chosen mouse out into the alley to die. That lying mouse then made his great strength vow a personal oath. They were sworn that not even a pip-squeak little one will survive their vengence. Now we come to the reason why we need to lure the Decoy into our cellar by way of a concert. During that cheese raid he slipped away to lay plans amongst the rotten fruit with that despicable Chosen one. We have found out, my friends, that the uncanny double has agreed to worm his way into our home, to cause disruption amongst us. He intended to excuse his absence by saying he had got lost on the night of the cheese raid. But Zero and I weren't fooled for a moment. We beat him to it by offering him a full pardon, and inviting him and his water-rat friends to entertain us tomorrow night. What mouse amongst you would not gladly throw himself upon the throat of that traitor-spy at this very moment? For what kind of cruel mice would plot to destroy our young ones?'

At this, some of the smaller mice began to whimper. Moments before they had been tossing lumps of coal at each other. Now they were filled with fear at the Sneak's words. So too were the rest of the Mob. The wily Sneak had done his work well. Only the one-eyed mouse and his friends remained unconvinced. But their scathing remarks were quickly drowned in the terrified hum that now echoed about the cellar.

'Now do you believe the awful things Zero's father said about his son?' yelled the triumphant Sneak. The loud 'yes' of the one-eyed mouse was howled down.

'And that is not all!' the Sneak shouted, the bit firmly between his teeth. 'Why do you think the Scout First Class slipped so quietly out of the cellar? Didn't you wonder about that?'

'I did,' piped his son. 'And now my dad, promoted into that traitor's post, is about to tell us why.'

'Because he too is part of the conspiracy!' the Sneak cried. 'He was on his way to shake paws with the Decoy who saved his life. That is why Zero and I were forced to act against that despicable Scout. Well, he won't betray us any more.'

'Now the truth's coming out,' muttered the one-eyed mouse. 'How many more mice will go missing before we wake up to what's going on? So the Scout is dead, and you killed him? So why did Zero not say this before? And why does he need you as his mouthpiece?'

'I was coming to that,' said the Sneak loudly. 'Grief is to blame for Zero's tongue-tied state. He is still mourning the treachery of the Scout and the death of his father, God bless him. He cannot trust himself to speak, can you, my leader?'

This was rubbish, of course. Zero was keeping quiet because he was having his bacon saved. Anyway, the Sneak's humdinger of a tale was beyond Zero's understanding. All he knew was the Sneak was getting him off the hook for some reason. Zero was quite satisfied to leave the verbalizing to his new partner in crime. For he had his own crude plans for that ambitious one. With the Mob behind him, Zero planned first to destroy the Decoy-singer, then pick off one by one the Chosen mouse and his strength as they came through the hole in the wall. Afterwards, when he no longer needed the Sneak, he would polish him off, thus stilling his too-clever tongue for ever.

'So!' yelled the Sneak, confident that he held the Mob in the palm of his paw. 'Are we all agreed the concert is a necessary evil that must go on? That the Decoy must die?'

'We agree,' nodded the confused mice. 'For we feel safer with devils we can see than saints we can't.'

The exceptions were the one-eyed mouse and his friends. Though they were prepared to fight any enemy of the Mob, they were yet to be convinced that the threat lay without. They believed with good reason that the real enemy was here in the Gas Street cellar. But they could only wait in readiness to oppose whomever sought to harm them.

The unhappy Gas Street Mob settled down for the night. But few would sleep. There would be much tossing and turning before Saturday morning dawned. The one-eyed mouse made no attempt to rest, but lay awake in wide-eyed thought the long hours through. Neither could the stupid bully-mice sleep. For some reason they couldn't understand, Zero had angrily snatched away their extra cheese-rations. With their stomachs gurgling so, sleep for them was impossible. But Zero slept. His was the sleep of the wicked. For the Devil, realising that his pay would soon be due, smoothed that wicked leader's brow and waited upon his soul.

Sleep did not find the Sneak. He also lay awake, his eyes glittering in the darkness. 'I always knew I had it in me to sway multitudes,' he whispered to himself. 'Just fancy, a lowly little mouse like me standing upon the threshhold of total power. Tremble, world, and with good cause, for I believe if I wasn't my own best friend, I would fear myself. . . . '

The Chosen mouse, hidden away in his hide of potato-peelings, heard all of this. And he was deeply angered. For he was no longer the idle, couldn't-care-less mouse of old. His stay on Lickey Top, although brief, and the slow journey back to the city with Fox, had forged a mouse worthy to be chosen for the task that lay ahead. He had seen how the mice of Lickey Top, despite their odd differences, had stuck loyally together for the good of all. And though at that time he had mocked their simplicity, he had come to envy the bond of warmth and mutual respect they shared. Now he understood their concern for the Pentecost mouse, who at this very moment went in fear for his life for the 'crimes' of daring to defend the Scout First Class, admitting to being a popular leader in his own right, and choosing to fight for his life when Zero had plotted his death. And then there had been the quiet influence of Fox. It was he who had forced the Chosen mouse to face and overcome his fears, frankly admitting his own by way of example. 'You will be cleansed inside and out . . . ' the old prophet had said, and so it had come about. Now the Chosen mouse was hurrying out of the city, crossing the great road, and breathlessly climbing the hill overlooking the city, where Fox waited. And Fox too was deeply angered as the mouse related his eavesdropping: the lies and the murky dealings. But then he listened quietly as the mouse told him his plan.

'It will involve great risk for you,' said a grave-faced Fox. Then he grinned comfortingly, for he could see the mouse was trying to hide the fear he naturally felt. He went on, 'But I won't be too far away. Between us we will pull if off, I'm sure.'

'Is it clear what you have to do, Fox?' asked the anxious mouse.

'As clear as daylight, little Chosen one in charge,' was the joking reply. 'Of course, we foxes being what we are I may improvise from time to time. Did you know I am prone to making sudden changes in direction for no particular reason? But I get your drift. But for now I have a little business to attend to. Did you happen to notice that fox-proof chicken wire we passed a short while back? Well, I'm willing to bet it isn't . . . fox-proof, I mean. Now don't worry, I won't be long. I'll see you early in the morning.'

'To see the last of you would break my heart,' said the Chosen mouse, his smile impish, though a mite strained. But his attempt to appear casual and unafraid was not completely successful. With Fox gone he had lots of time to think. Time and again through that dark night he fought to shrug away his doubts and fears. But those old enemies were still his companions when dawn broke. . . .

12 Bridge over Troubled Waters

Down in the Gas Street Basin all was quiet and still. This backwater place seemed to be still slumbering in an age-old dream of bustle and the ghosts of plodding horses, floating coals to far-off places. But if carefully sought, there was life here in the Basin. Even now small dramas were taking place. The gnats, enjoying the late sun, swarmed in their thousands above the waters of the canal. They were not alone. From a crevice in the tow-path wall, two tired eyes watched their gyrations. At the same time a greying old snout moved silently. Two paws, enfeebled by age, twiddled there in the gloom. Totting and counting, only to start again, they had taken on an impossible task. For the insects were too many, they flew so fast, and there was not the time . . . never the time . . . .

All night and day long, a broken-hearted old mouse had sat gazing out over the canal, reviewing his past life. Sometimes he smiled, though wistfully. Often his eyes would light with pride. For who could deny that in his time he had been a wise and good leader of the Gas Street Mob? Then his spirits would droop again. It was to take his mind off unpleasant thoughts that he had attempted to count those swirling gnat clouds. But as the afternoon advanced and his totals became more confused, he was wishing they would depart, and leave him in peace. Soon the darkness and that which stalked it would claim him. When dusk fell it was his intention to emerge from the crevice and wait for Black Shadow to take him from this life. For what was there to live for now? He had denounced his own son. He had branded as a villain the one he should love best. Those were his thoughts as he turned his weary head to the wall, and waited the slow passing of time. . . .

Just before the sun set, a hastening mouse was entering the city once more. Soon he arrived at his destination, the Gas Street Basin.

'Psst.' The voice was soft, but urgent. A quivering and whiskered nose was thrust into the crevice. Startled, the old mouse scrunched deeper into his hide, eyes wary at the sight of the intruder. Then recognition dawned. For who could mistake that brown and white pelt, those strangely flopping ears?

'You do remember me?' came the hoarse whisper.

'I recall a mouse who once broke the oath of the Gas Street Mob,' came the muzzy reply, tinged faintly with anger. Then confusedly, 'But there was another. He claimed to be Chosen, then went away. . . . '

'I am that mouse,' urged the other. 'The Chosen one who was thrown to Black Shadow by your son, and lived to tell the tale.'

'I have no son,' said the old mouse, shaking his head. 'I once had a friend, I dimly recall. He was known as Zero the Stubborn. He had a son, I believe. But this son turned out bad. . . . He was evil. . . . He caused my friend much pain. . . . '

'This friend . . . this Zero the Stubborn?' pressed the Chosen mouse. 'Did he, in his time, consider the welfare of his Mob above all things?'

'He did,' was the sighed reply.

'And would he have acted to save that Mob from the

clutches of a tyrant, even though that tyrant be his own son?'

'In all honour, yes,' whispered the old one. His paws cupped to receive a bowed head. The Chosen mouse continued, but gently. He had no wish to distress the other more than he could help. He was aware that somehow this old leader had blotted from his mind the kinship that existed between him and his son. This illusion, however, was fragile. Questioned too harshly, and the old mouse's self-protective retreat from shame could easily crumble, and destroy whatever sanity remained in that poor, worn brain. 'This Zero the Stubborn, who is no longer with us,' probed the Chosen one. 'With his great experience he would have been familiar with every secret twist and turn of the Gas Street Basin? He might even have known of a way to cross the canal without risk of drowning?'

Pride fought with sadness as the old mouse replied. 'He bridged those troubled waters many times, in the days of scampering youth.'

'So if he were here he could lead me directly to that secret place?' said the Chosen mouse. His voice became softly cajoling. 'Pretend you are he, lead me there. I am sure your friend would approve, were he here to speak.'

Slowly, as if in a trance, the grey-whiskered oldster emerged from the crevice. He seemed unaware of the presence of the Chosen mouse as he limped off down the tow-path, in the direction of the tunnel. Soon they had entered its echoing gloom. Save for a glimmer of light from the farther end, it was a dark, forbidding place. Water dripped unceasingly from the arched and slimy brickwork, loud in the ears as it hit the water in random patterns of gulps and plops. Now the old mouse had stopped to examine a section of wall. A slight hesitation, and he was squeezing into a narrow gap. The Chosen mouse scrambled along behind. Now they were inside the wall of the tunnel itself. Then began an awkward and upward climb, the mice threading their way through the heaps of rotted mortar that had once bound the courses of brick together. Zig-zagging this way and that, the secret passage-way soon began to curve over. Once, stopping for breath, the Chosen mouse glanced down through a crack between his paws, and saw the black gleam of water below. Moving on, they soon began to descend again. Moments later they were emerging from a similar hole on the farther bank, the canal safely bridged. Though so recently in charge, the old mouse quickly lapsed back into his former, bewildered state. Dejectedly, he slumped against the wall, his paws listlessly twiddling, a blank and empty stare in his eyes.

The Chosen mouse reached out a gentle paw, and spoke above the din of falling water. 'This Zero the Stubborn?' he said, compassion in his tone. 'Would he not yearn for the company of his family at this time? Would he return to the Gas Street cellar if he believed that in the goodness of time, a Chosen mouse would banish evil, and forge amongst the Mob a sense of honour and justice once more? Would he trust in the word of such a mouse? Would he, on those terms, return home and take up once again a still useful life?'

'He could not,' came the broken reply. 'For the evil to be cast out is forever part of him. The old mouse we speak of died long ago inside. He would prefer to remain here and meet his fate, content in the knowledge that those he leaves behind will live in peace and happiness. Ah, but that friend of mine could count so nimbly in those days. Once he totalled the stars in the sky, and they all winking with mischief . . . . You are a Chosen mouse, you say? Then do what you must do, the blessing of an old leader would go with you if he were here to speak. . . . '

For one brief moment they looked into each other's eyes. One pair was bright, though sad; the old mouse's sad, though bright with tears. The Chosen mouse then turned away. The respect he felt for the other prompted him to say no more. Soon he was hurrying out of the tunnel in the direction of the half-sunken narrow-boat, from where the sound of up-raised voices could be plainly heard. Though filled with compassion, he did not look back.

'When you're down . . . ' warbled the right side-kick, '. . . feeling small . . . ' '. . . When tears are in your eyes . . . I'll dry them all . . . ' sang his friend sweetly.

The water-rats had become more and more excited as dusk approached. In contrast, Pentecost became increasingly desperate. But as the sun disappeared, a feeling of dull acceptance came over him. Fox would not come. Fox did not wish to come, the mouse finally realised. And who could blame him? No-one had tried harder than him to make the mouse see sense, and to stay home where he belonged. But Pentecost had felt compelled to go. Did not the Old Codger say he must? But the mouse had experienced nothing but confusion in the city. Since teaming up with the water-rats he had gone over and over in his mind just what the old hedgehog's gift had prophesied. Here in the city he was supposed to meet with one who, with Pentecost's help, would overthrow a wicked tyrant. So where was that 'soulmate' whose destiny was so closely bound with his own? But the question was unnecessary, for Pentecost knew very well where he was. The bug had spelled it out quite plainly. Instead of teaming up with Pentecost to fight the evils in the city, this double, the Chosen mouse, had teamed up with Fox in the safety of the hills. So much for the Old Codger's gift, for it had certainly proved false on that point. But a much chastened Pentecost could only bitterly agree on another. The gift had foretold of a mouse returning. A mouse who would not be what he seemed. Foolishly, Pentecost had paid little heed to those words. But now, gazing forlornly out over the darkening Basin, he was in no doubt as to their meaning. The returning and unseemly mouse was never meant to be him. The Chosen mouse was the one destined to be the cause of great . . . the gift could only have meant 'great rejoicing', for had not the bug said how made for each other Fox and the Chosen mouse seemed? As for the rest, Pentecost could only grieve and regret. His family had disowned and outlawed him, and had chosen to appoint Uncle in his place. So all in all, what had he to live for now? Filled with these depressing thoughts, Pentecost finally accepted his lot, and prepared to meet his end in the Gas Street cellar. . . .

The Basin Swingers were readying themselves to go. For a few moments they left the mouse to himself, as with excited and trembling paws they scooped up fresh water from the deck and gargled vigorously. Watching them, Pentecost, even at this grave moment, was moved by their innocent joy. Certain that they stood on the threshold of fame and fortune, they whooped and splashed, and danced a slippery jig upon the deck of the narrow-boat. . . .

'Not a word,' hissed a voice. Pentecost's cry of surprise was quickly stifled by a rough paw. At the same

time he was dragged unceremoniously behind a coil of rope. Wildly, Pentecost attempted to turn his head to view his attacker. He was warned to be still and quiet. The voice, low and urgent, continued. 'If you value your life, listen. Time is short, so do exactly as I tell you. No questions, just listen. . . .'

Moments later a brown and white mouse was swarming over the side of the boat and was bowling, head-down and ears flopping, in the direction of the tunnel. A hole was sought, and quickly found. A frantic scramble and he was clambering upwards, choking on the powdered mortar raised by his desperate passage. In no time he had bridged the canal and was scurrying along, searching . . . searching . . . . The crevice gained, he huddled inside, chest heaving as he fought for breath. Now his mind was a mixed confusion of fear and hope – but especially hope. For he was remembering the brief words of his rescuer before being urged to flee: 'Fox is on his way. Don't stir until you hear him howl – that is the signal. Take heart, for though we share these fears, we share a friend in Fox, too.'

13 Black Shadow

A tongue, pink and wet, polished and sleeked until fur shone gloss-white. A sinuous spine arched and stretched, and a mouth yawned wide into a sharp sneer. Then down from the heights came Black Shadow, toes casually nimble as he sprang from tiled roof to sagging out-house, from glass-topped wall to cobble-stone. Softly, almost tenderly, his cushioned paws sped him through the night-time city. *His* city, for this place had been designed for such as he. As the jungle for the tiger, so the cold concrete subways and alleys of the town were Black Shadow's haunts and trails. Here he could prey on the small creatures who hurried through those echoing places. Here he could despatch vicious business, the cries of terror to no avail, for the city turned its back and slept, dreaming of the morning.

Pad, pad, Black Shadow sped quietly along. He was late abroad tonight, had overslept, but there was no hurry. By dusk he had reached the heart of the city and was entering one of the many subways, the rumble of the traffic growing fainter as he descended. Suddenly he stopped, and crouched, his eyes and ears tuned to the soft sounds of his underground kingdom. For a while he lay concealed in the shadows, just outside the headquarters of the Queensway Mob. His patience was not rewarded. Doubtless that band had already set out on a raid, hence the absence of activity. Disappointed, he rose and moved on. Soon he was emerging from the warren-like subways into bright street-lights. Swiftly

darting across a busy road, he gained the security of the shadows once more. Creeping along, he took a right and then a left turn, to arrive at his next stake-out. This time he was in luck. There was a scuffle, a sharp cry, and a Broad Street Decoy took his leave of life. Blooded and satisfied, Black Shadow sloped off in the direction of Gas Street. . . .

'Why, if it isn't old snowball!' jeered a voice from above. 'To think our pretty puss is your actual terror of the night!'

For a split second Black Shadow paused and stiffened. Then he was stalking on, looking directly ahead and plainly determined to ignore the pin-point of orange light that had appeared from nowhere, to dance attendance about his ears.

'So we are the fabled Black Shadow?' sneered the cockle-snorkle. 'So who do you think you're kidding, snowy? So who's got our tongue . . . ?'

Black Shadow stopped, his tongue pink and quick as he lapped from an oily puddle. The glow from the circling bug caused his reflection to appear ghostly lemon. The king of the city did not linger; the bug, angered that he should be so ignored, followed, his steady stream of insults and taunts making not the slightest impression on his intended victim. He was yet to find out that, unlike all other creatures, the white cat could not be reached, whether through flattery or ridicule. The wall of silence Black Shadow had built about himself was unbreachable, for he was beholden to no one. But the bug was stubborn. Everyone had a chink in their armour. It was simply a question of finding it. He tried the friendly and helpful approach.

'Have you heard about the concert in the Gas Street cellar tonight? Now if you were to hurry, you could pounce and prey to your heart's content, for if I'm not mistaken, the Basin must be a regular little beehive at this moment. I'm telling you, Gas Street is where the action is tonight. So what do you say, my old white tornado, interest stirring, is it?'

The bug could have kicked himself with a spare leg as he said those words. For almost immediately Black Shadow was spinning around, was stalking back towards the city centre. Too late the bug realised he had made a grave mistake. He had offered advice to one who walked alone. In so doing he almost certainly saved the lives of a singing quartet, who at that very moment were crossing the canal, to keep a date in the Gas Street cellar.

'You dare ignore me?' screamed the frustrated bug, his wrath expressing itself in an explosion of violent orange light. He dived and bombed about Black Shadow's ears, his words a torrent of spite and malice. 'Look at me, you stupid green-eyed simpleton. Don't you realise who I am? Nine lives? You pride yourself with having nine lives? Let me tell you this, one day when you are a set of tortured violin strings and a pair of warm gloves, I'll still be bustling in this world. For I will live for ever . . . for ever, do you hear me?' The bug's voice rose to an hysterical shriek as Black Shadow, without so much as a glance, slipped out of sight and earshot around a city corner.

Fuming, the bug set off for the Gas Street Basin. He arrived not to a busy beehive of comings and goings, but to a silence and a stillness one could have cut with a knife. Only the now-settling waters of the canal gave hint that but recently a quartet had passed that way, to keep a rendezvous with destiny. The bug, his ego in shreds, perched upon the tow-path wall, allowing his heated temper to cool. So absorbed in repairing his shattered pride was he, he failed to notice the furtive movement directly below. Ordinarily, his keen eyes would not have missed that merest tip of whiskered nose that poked out from the crevice in the wall, to withdraw just as quickly. But the bug was not his confident and all-seeing self at that moment. So now what, he thought, preening his wings. He considered his priorities. Should he go see how Fox and the Chosen mouse were faring? Or should he proceed at once to the Gas Street cellar, to view the misery of the Pentecost mouse? And then there was Lickey Top. Had he time to nip home to give that bubbling cauldron a quick stir? His excitement mounted as he became his old exuberant self. Priorities, priorities, who would be a bug with so much to do, and so little time to do it . . . ? Triumphantly, he opened his wings and leapt into the air. 'Wings over the world!' he yelled, not knowing, for the moment, and caring less, where his frantic dash might lead him. . . .

14 The Struggle for Power

Dripping wet, his ears bedraggled and drooping over his eyes, the small mouse stood on firmly planted paws in a puddle of smelly canal water. Slowly he glanced around the ring of apprehensive and hostile faces. For a moment his gaze lingered on a tiny group who sat somewhat apart. Their expressions were querying rather than accusing. For the one-eyed Breaker and his friends wished to hear the newcomer's side of the story before condemning. The bug had certainly been right when he had said to Zero and the Sneak that the talents of the water-rats would prove too large for the Gas Street cellar. . . .

A short time after dusk, the Basin Swingers Quartet arrived in Gas Street, as promised. Being a little late, the water-rats in their eagerness hadn't bothered to shake themselves off after their swim across the canal. They had raced up the alley-way, dragging the small mouse with them, water cascading from their fur and pooling over the cobbles. Enthusiastically shoving their contralto forward, they attempted to squeeze into the cellar after him. A fool could have told them they wasted their time. The right side-kick, the smallest of the three, managed to get his head inside before becoming firmly stuck about the ears. After some grunting and wriggling he withdrew, the left side-kick immediately taking his place. Only after they had persuaded King to have a try did the awful truth begin to dawn. Because of a too-small booking and an excess of talent, fickle fame had kicked them in the teeth yet again. Forlornly, the right side-kick called through the hole to suggest that, as it was such a pleasant evening, perhaps an open-air concert would fit the bill? They were the modern rage, he explained, hopefully.

'What, with Black Shadow likely to turn up at any moment?' yelled Zero. 'Not on your life. The concert is cancelled, so hop it.'

'Then would you please return our contralto?' said the left side-kick, a sob in his voice. 'For without him all our hopes for a come-back will gurgle down the drain.'

'Contralto?' sneered the Sneak. 'The only gurgling we are interested in is when this criminal Decoy slips down Black Shadow's throat. So what are you hanging about for, you washed-up has-beens? On your way, for losers give me the creeps.'

The water-rats squelched miserably away, their dreams of a bright show business future as far away as the stars that began to shine through the broken cloud above. Soon they were back where they started, aboard the narrow-boat down in the Basin, crooning their blues, two pairs of eyes filled with sadness and gazing into the empty ones of their beloved King. . . .

'Criminal, oath-breaking mouse. So you planned to join up with the Chosen mouse, eh?' were Zero's bellowed opening remarks. He was glaring mad-eyed at the captive. 'Well, you treacherous deserting Decoy, your plan came unstuck. Your mistake was to accept my phoney full pardon and concert offer. A mouse with his head out of the clouds would have known it was a trap. So now you are to be disposed of, as will be the Chosen mouse and his great strength when they arrive from the countryside quite near the Bull Ring. And don't think we can't do it, for there is one thing I'll bet the Chosen mouse hasn't thought of. There is only room enough for one invader at a time to slip through that hole in the wall. As you will be rubbed out singly, so will they when they arrive. And don't think you can squirm off the hook, for there isn't a mouse Jack in this cellar who will lift a paw to help you.'

'You are mistaken to call me Decoy!' shouted the prisoner in ringing tones. 'For I have never held such a post. In fact I have never held down a job in my life. But before this night is out I mean to be fully employed, though certainly not as a Decoy. When I have made my rousing speech the Mob will be in no doubt as to where my talents lie. Look closely, now do you see who I am?'

'Please don't glance at me when you ask that,' begged the Sneak. 'For the awful truth is beginning to dawn.'

'What truth?' snapped Zero, still not understanding.

'And still you do not recognise me!' cried the mouse. 'Well, I will jog your memory. I am he you so feared as a rival, and tried to be rid of. I am that mouse who so annoyed you that you secretly threw me to Black Shadow. Little did you know that from the moment I met my old prophet on Spaghetti Junction, I was under the protection of destiny itself. Tremble, Zero, bloody tyrant, for I have been chosen to bring about your downfall, and wrest the Mob from their bondage. I am not that poor persecuted Decoy, but the Chosen mouse.'

'Heaven bless us!' yelled the Mob as one. 'It is a miracle!'

'Now we have our leader!' shouted the jubilant one-eyed mouse. 'And what a change of personality his wandering in the wilderness has brought about. Gone are his pithy remarks, and his irritating tossing of deftly-caught cheese. Instead, the Chosen mouse returns to stand nobly before us, simmering with a quiet fire, and fairly oozing leadership qualities. My friends and I have long awaited such a mouse. We take our stand beside him. He need only make a sign, and Zero and his hangers-on will be no more.' Instantly, he and his friends rose to take their stand at the side of the Chosen mouse.

'Traitors!' screamed a terrified Zero. But he was by no means finished. Viciously, he motioned for his bully-mice to rally close and then snapped out a command to the Sneak. The response from that mouse was to snuggle deeper amidst the crush.

'Can't you see I am swinging like an anxious pendulum?' he cried. 'Though I love you dearly, yet I also feel affection for the Chosen mouse. Is it my fault I have too many friends to hold dear?'

Zero reacted just as the Sneak hoped. Seeing himself deserted on every side, the leader began to rant and storm. All the goading and the fear had turned him into a dangerous mouse indeed. He would fight blindly and to the death now, thought the contented Sneak. But before things went any further, a very important question remained unanswered. Had not the little orange bug cautioned them that the Chosen mouse was returning with a great strength? So where lurked that force?

It was obvious Zero was now pondering that same problem. For the leader was dashing about like a mouse demented, his paws pounding a sweaty trail between his bully-mice, and the hole in the wall. 'Stand fast!' he bellowed. Then on winged toes he flew to peer out into the night. His feverish eyes deceived him. 'They're out there!' he screamed, through whiskers bedraggled with the dampness of fear. 'I see my enemies flitting like taunting shadows beneath the ghostly moon. Why do they not show themselves, and fight the Mob like true mice? Why do they steal softly amongst the dustbins, their blood-thirsty chuckles echoing about the grim, prison-like walls of the brooding alley-way?'

The Chosen One looked every inch the mouse in shining armour as he gazed at a panting Zero. Paws akimbo, head thrown proudly back, he spoke, contempt in his tone. 'I have not come mob-handed to overthrow you,' he said. 'For my ally is here in the cellar. I have no need of numbers, when right is on my side.'

For one brief moment, the one-eyed mouse and his friends appeared to falter. At the same time Zero's savage heart gave a leap. Was it some trick? Or had the Chosen mouse really returned alone? If so, Zero was still in with a chance, but he knew he must act immediately. He was just about to prod and goad his bullies into action when the Chosen mouse spoke again. This time his words were addressed to the one-eyed mouse. The Mob craned to pick up the quiet exchange between the two, as did a bewildered Zero. But the Chosen mouse was no longer the loud-mouthed braggart they had once known. Whatever was said, the Mob could only agree that the words of the Chosen mouse must have been noble ones; for, after a slight hesitation, the one-eyed mouse and his friends left his side. Soon they were seating themselves amongst the close-packed mice.

The attention of everyone in the cellar was now centred upon Zero and the Chosen mouse now standing face to face. Zero, his eyes filled with hatred, was trying to summon up the courage to lunge, to make an end of the other. He realised that this was the crunch. The next few moments would decide whether he continued his harsh rule or fell – either in death, or to that place he feared most: the bottom of the heap. Unflinchingly, the Chosen mouse waited for his enemy to make his move. Though he was prepared to fight, his hope was that Zero would crumble, admit his many crimes, and throw himself on the mercy of forgiving friends. And perhaps in time even *his* evil soul could be redeemed.

But the ambitious Sneak was having none of it. His eyes looked anything but saintly at this moment. Glittering with an unholy and terrifying cunning, they stared fixedly at the contestants. He began to shout, hoping that his oily words would touch off the spark that would set mouse against mouse, the fire spreading until the whole of the cellar became consumed in an orgy of violence and destruction. 'The cowards hesitate!' he cried. 'Are they only brave with words? Friends, comrades, city mice, let's get this clear, there will be no peace in this cellar until the power-lusting Zero and the Chosen mouse have settled their differences with a good old-fashioned up-and-downer. Only when they have destroyed each other can we drag from our group that shy mouse who will lead us towards a better future. But please ignore my plain and fair straight-down-the-line speaking, for I wish only to exist as a quietly monkish mouse. Never, ever, will I rise to your cheers, and serve you all my days. . . .'

These words from the Sneak, of all mice, were enough to make an honest mouse choke on his cheese-ration. Had the Mob heard him right? The Sneak was offering himself for the leadership, and before it was vacant too? Only now did the Mob realise the full extent of that odious mouse's ambition. Long had they tolerated his spine-tingling sucking-up and crawling to mice in high positions. He had even got away with framing various mice whose jobs he desired. But this was too much. Their feelings were expressed by a young mouse who quickly scrambled to his feet.

'You fiend!' he cried, shaking a paw in the face of the now hooded-eyed Sneak. 'What makes you think you could ever qualify for the leadership of the Gas Street Mob?'

'Well, for one, I'm out of a job at the moment,' replied the Sneak hopefully. 'And for another, anyone can see how popular I've become lately. Unlike two other mice I could mention, I am a mouse of peace.'

'Liar!' shouted the young mouse hotly. He turned and

addressed the family. 'You know me as the son of the Scout First Class, mysteriously vanished. Like my missing father, high spirits are lost on me. But honour makes me the steadiest of rocks. Though I refuse the affection of the Mob, I can demand their respect and attention.'

'Indeed that is true,' murmured the one-eyed mouse. 'So speak on, little friend, forever lost to us.'

The Scout's son pointed at Zero and the Chosen mouse. Though warily watching each other, still they hesitated to close in combat. Like the rest of the Mob they listened as the youngster spoke on.

'Are we to stand quietly by whilst the leader we have long awaited is killed before our eyes? Let us rise up and stop this insanity. Let us decide our own destiny. Let us with one accord joyfully acclaim the returned Chosen mouse as our leader. Let us with one stern roar, disclaim the evil Zero, and banish him from our midst for ever. . . .'

The words of the lonely mouse went straight to the hearts of the Mob. Immediately they were rising to mill about their champion Chosen mouse. Zero stood alone and ignored. The Mob, truly united at last, no longer feared him. And because his only weapon, the fear he had instilled in others, had been struck from his grasp, he now stood his true self, a naked and empty shell. Carefully, the Sneak avoided him. He had no wish to become associated with a loser. He realised his own bid for power had failed, at least this time. But he was confident his chance would come again. In the meantime his reaction was to save his own skin by lustily leading the cheers for the Chosen mouse. He even had the nerve to call for order, that he might say a few words. Excited and laughing, he held up a paw in an appeal for silence.

'Yes, we are all delighted,' he agreed, nodding his head, and smiling his special sickly smile. 'And may I say, there is no one more delighted than I. What our beloved new leader needs now is a right-hand mouse to take the pressure off him. Well, if his warm promoting paw should fall on me, I can only do my best. But now I expect he is aching to chide the Mob for misunderstanding me? While he does, I will sit humbly in the corner. Pardon me as I slip away . . . .' He turned, the yellow streak down his back rippling as he sped to hide beneath the roof-tile in the corner.

'Slip away you certainly will!' thundered the Chosen mouse. 'For you are a criminal of the worst kind. But first you will answer a few questions concerning the mysterious disappearance of the Scout First Class.'

'It wasn't me, it was Zero who did for him,' came a wail from the corner. 'I tried to stop Zero, but he was in a maddened rage.'

Suddenly the bug came scorching into the cellar from somewhere or other. He alighted on a rafter and looked down in surprise. 'What's this?' he said. 'The Pentecost Decoy in charge? I don't believe it. Last time I saw him he was sweating out his last few hours. Now look at him. All noble, and in total command. What a turn-up. So he won't be needing my help, after all. . . .'

'But I do,' quavered the Sneak from his corner. 'Please tell the Chosen mouse that I am an innocent party in all this. Everyone has turned on me now. I haven't a friend in the world but you.'

'And not even me,' breezed the bug, glowing contentedly. 'Didn't I warn you I was liable to change sides upon a whim? Well, I have. I am now firmly on the side of the Pentecost Decoy – Chosen mouse? What do you mean – Chosen mouse?'

The new leader glanced up at the bug in distaste. 'A lot has happened since we last met. No thanks to you I did return, and Zero stands overthrown, and is now banished. The Pentecost mouse you mistake me for is in a safe place, waiting for the arrival of his friend Fox. Yes, you tried hard to frustrate us, nasty little bug, but we have triumphed in spite of you.'

'Well, what a turn-up,' breathed the bug, admiringly. 'So you pulled a switch, eh? How come I missed that? I must be slipping. So where is the Pentecost mouse? But never mind, I'll soon flush him out. I have to help Fox return him home in safety. And if you believe that, you'll believe anything. But hurry up, for I'm impatient to see how you deal with this miserable pair.' Folding away his wings and winking out his light, he settled to watch the unfolding scene below.

'Let it be known that from this moment forth the tyrant Zero and the odious Sneak are banished from the Gas Street cellar forever!' shouted the Chosen mouse in ringing tones. 'It is their punishment that they will be turned out to take their chances in the city. That, I might add, is more lenient a treatment than I and the Scout First Class received. So depart I say, in the name of God go, for the sight of you sickens us.'

'So you banish me?' hissed Zero, the naked hatred in his close-set eyes causing many a mouse to shudder and cringe away. But though his venom was real, his next words were bluff and wishful thinking. Shuffling across to the hole in the wall, black fur moulting all over the floor, he turned and spat. 'One day I'll be back, and with a great and terrible strength of my own. And when I do return, not a one of you will survive my vengeful wrath. So, all of you, toss and turn in your sleep, for the nightmare of my coming will be sooner than you think.' With that he stepped out into the night and was gone.

The Sneak had been trembling throughout. Peeping from beneath the tile he watched with foreboding the departure of Zero. Now it was his turn. It seemed that his worming, fawning days were over. Yet despite his predicament, ambition still ruled him. As he shrinkingly surveyed the host of accusing faces that stared his way, an idea began to germinate. An impossible idea, but yet . . . . Like a flash he hurried across to the hole, easily beating Zero's old five-second rule as he gained the darkness of the alley-way.

'Now what do you think he's up to?' said the curious bug. 'His sneaky type always begs for another chance. So why didn't he? Why does he beat a hasty retreat as if he knows exactly where he's going? I must keep tabs on that one.'

'Has anyone ever told you to mind your own business?' said the Chosen mouse sharply.

'Often,' admitted the insect. 'But I don't take much notice. Anyway, this *is* my business. I'm in it up to my neck. So this is my agenda. First I intend to find out what happens to the banished baddies, and then the boring bit, I'll pop back and give the goodies a pat on the back, for I expect Fox and the Pentecost mouse will put in an appearance before too long. You'll excuse me then, for if ever a mouse intrigued me, it's that sneaky one. I'll see you when I see you . . . .'

He flew down from the rafter, and made to skim out of the cellar. Too late he noticed the shimmering spider's web, cunningly draped from wall to floor. In a trice he was spread-eagled and trapped at its centre, his frantic struggles to free himself merely binding him faster. 'Don't just stand there!' he yelled between gasps.

'Get me out of this. For believe me, old hairy-legs will know not what he does. We can't expect him to appreciate my extreme rarity. Don't you realise I'm an endangered species?'

'It certainly looks like it,' replied the Chosen mouse drily. 'Do you really think we would lift a paw to help you after all the trouble you've caused?'

The spider, who appeared out of his nest to view his latest catch, was not impressed by the bug's outburst. To his mind, all bugs were endangered if he had anything to do with it. He saw not a valuable trophy, but breakfast, plain and simple. Like a high-wire artist, he stretched out an exceedingly hairy leg, as if in preparation for his act. Seeing this, the bug began to tear at the sticky gossamer strands.

The mice were breathlessly watching the tiny drama. Many felt pity for the impudent little insect. But then they didn't know him, nor realise the mischief he had caused. The Chosen mouse soon put them straight.

'Some of you might think me a vindictive mouse,' he said. 'But I will tell you this: though that beautiful bug is not an actual murderer, he is not above dipping his wings in the blood spilled by others. For I came to know him well out in the countryside. I saw how he delighted to wallow in the misery of others. Because of his meddling, my mission to return and overthrow Zero was almost frustrated. Heaven knows what other criminal plots he is responsible for. Well, for once in his life he is now trapped and cowed. But to prove I am not a vindictive leader, I am prepared to offer that wicked bug a chance to live. If he can prove to us that there is one person in the whole wide world who cares a fig for him, he can go free.'

For one brief moment the spider paused in his advance. His glittering eyes gazed deep into those of the bug's. Whatever he saw there could not have been to the cockle-snorkle's advantage. Slowly, on long and delicately balancing legs, he began again his mincing walk to the hub of his web. The bug's despairing glow guttered out. He was a realist if nothing else. For indeed, who cared a jot for him? In all honesty, he could think of no-one at this time – nor any other time for that matter. Yet though he had no wish to die, the Gas Street Mob would hear no more begging for help from him. He owed it to his rare species and the world in general to die with dignity. For there would surely be a universal outcry when the news broke that there was one less cockle-snorkle on earth. And when the great, fat, and heavy books were written about him, he wished the story to end thus: 'And so passed from the earth an extremely rare, seven-legged, oranged-backed cockle-snorkle, who died with a bang, not a whimper. . . . ' Glum, though prepared, the bug stole a glance at his high-stepping executioner. Was that a glimmer of affection in the spider's eyes? Could old hairy-legs turn out to be the one who cared a fig for him? But the bug knew he was kidding himself. Doubtless before the morning broke he would be a dried-up husk, beginning to gather the dust of ages. Oh well, sighed the bug to himself, we all have our problems, eh . . . ?

15 The Quality of Mercy

Pad, pad, freeze: Black Shadow stole quietly along the canal tow-path. The city centre had proved disappointingly deserted. Now he was returning to his favourite hunting ground, Gas Street. Glad to have shaken off the irritating bug, the lonely stroll through the shadowy streets had been most relaxing. For a moment he leaned out over the waters of the canal, purring with pleasure to see the reflected menace in his eyes. Soon he moved on, past the small crevice in the wall where Pentecost dozed fitfully, waiting the arrival of Fox. The great cat stalked on, his paws firm and sure on the narrow concrete strip that bounded the still waters. A sudden shower of sparks from the chimney-pipe of a narrow-boat lit up the Basin with a ruddy glow, the fragments falling spitting and spent upon the oily black depths. Softly from the farther bank came floating the sound of lamenting voices, one deep and sad, the others trebled and blending.

Pad, pad, freeze again: now Black Shadow was crouching, his muscles tensed, his tail switching. He could scarcely believe his luck. For shambling towards him was a scruffy black mouse, his head sunk into his chest as if deep in thought. He seemed to be in a trance-like state as he wove along that concrete strip. Once he lost his balance, almost toppling over into the murky waters. Somehow he recovered, to stagger on. Another display of sparks illuminated the Basin. Now Black Shadow could see the dull and moulting fur, the sleepwalker's eyes of his victim. Eagerly the great cat closed, and struck out with a vicious paw. The mouse, alert now, recoiled in horror. His cry of fear awakened Pentecost. By the light of the dying sparks he watched through wide and startled eyes as Zero desperately sought to escape those lashing claws. Then suddenly another figure appeared. Racing along the canal came Fox, his jaws snapping as Black Shadow, surprised and distracted from his prey, spun around to defend himself. The usually gentle Fox was transformed into the merciless killer, for in his blind fury he saw not Zero quaking there, but his best friend the Pentecost mouse. His teeth bit deep, tearing into the snarling cat's flank, and Black Shadow, having once tasted Fox's fury, broke away and fled once more like the coward he was. Their abrupt departure caused Zero to stumble. With a loud cry he toppled over the edge of the concrete strip, his paws frantically clutching at the grasses that grew between the cracks. His grip held. And there he hung, his toes brushing the water, his eyes wide, as with a tearing sound the brittle grasses began to part, one by one.

Pentecost had watched that grim drama in a state of frozen horror. Now he collected himself to spring into action. Quickly he was out of the crevice and scurrying across to the water's edge. Leaning over, he looked down into the beseeching gaze of Zero. Suddenly Pentecost, his compassion aroused, saw not the enemy who had sought to destroy him. Below, clinging to life, he saw only a fellow creature in distress. Swiftly, wordlessly, he reached down to grab a pawful of Zero's fur, his rear paws scrabbling for purchase as he strove to pull the other to safety. At that moment the last grass stem gave way. Now all that prevented Zero slipping down to a watery grave was the firm clutch of his would-be rescuer. Still neither one uttered a sound, yet their eyes remained locked. There was puzzlement in Zero's fixed stare, despite the fear in his heart, for he had recognised his saviour and could not understand. For what kind of mouse was this who would help a foe as he would a friend? During those final moments Zero did come to comprehend. His eyes seemed to plead for forgiveness as his rotting fur tore away, and he sank beneath the oily waters of the canal, leaving Pentecost still clutching at that pathetic clump of hair. Silkily the waters calmed. The only signs that a wicked life had been snuffed out in those peaceful surrounds were a few grass stems idling upon the water. The singing from the farther bank had ceased during those moments of savagery and merciful struggle. Now it resumed again, sweet and melodious, drifting through the Gas Street Basin, that tucked-away place where time seemed to always stand still. . . .

The regret at the passing of a life was replaced by a feeling of relief and joy. Pentecost was realising that he had never truly been alone in his misery. He should have known that he had been ever in the thoughts of Fox. And now his friend had come back for him. The heart of the Pentecost mouse was light and singing as he set off towards the only refuge he could think of, the Gas Street cellar. There he would await the second coming of his friend, Fox of Furrowfield. As soon as Black Shadow had been seen off Fox would return, of this the mouse had not the slightest doubt. . . .

Seeing Pentecost enter the cellar, one or two mice made threatening moves towards him.

'Stop!' cried the Chosen mouse, leaping across to protect his sorely-tried double. 'Can't you see who this is?'

'And while you're about it you can stop this one!' yelled the bug, jerking his head at the nearing spider. 'So the Pentecost mouse is safe and sound. So who will smother me with warmth? Surely someone will sympathise with my dire straits?'

His plight was ignored. The Chosen mouse, assisted by the one-eyed Breaker, helped the tired mouse across the cellar. Gently they sat him down upon a mound of soft soot and began to question him. But Pentecost was in no mood to speak. Although safe at last, he had witnessed and experienced many terrible things in the city, and wished only to be left alone for a while. He could think clearly now, and was able to come to terms with himself. He had set out for the city in the hope of becoming a hero in his own right, and he had failed. It was never meant to be. For he realised now that he had been but a lowly pawn in destiny's plan. His role had been to suffer that the Chosen mouse might return to lead the city mice towards a better future. And it had all come to pass. For, raising his head, he saw that Chosen one, no longer boastfully idle, but proudly erect and clearly worshipped. And to bring this about, it was Pentecost who had paid the price. For since entering the city he had been subjected to many indignities. He had cowered in hiding in the cellar; had pleaded for his life upon emerging; had humbly accepted a suicidal Decoy post; had been, during the cheese raid, chased and almost killed by Black Shadow; and again, to preserve his skin, had agreed to become a failure by joining an unknown singing group. In short he had been harried and bullied from pillar to post, and had hardly ever lifted a paw in protest. He, Pentecost of Lickey Top, had been reduced to a running, hiding, nodding mouse, and now he felt terribly ashamed. And finally, though he was thankful that Fox had come back for him, it was a bitter thought that he would soon be returning home, not as an equal hero, but as a chastened and cowed runaway.

Then a voice was speaking. The words did not confirm Pentecost's own opinion at all. With mounting astonishment and happiness, Pentecost listened as the son of the late Scout First Class began to sing his praises. 'I am honoured to meet again that mouse who spoke up in defence of my father,' he was saying. 'And though that brave Scout is no longer with us, I am sure that somewhere he pauses in his blazing of fresh trails, and thinks coolly of you.'

The one-eyed Breaker arose to express his own thoughts. 'Never will I forget how you thrashed Zero within an inch of his life,' he declared admiringly. 'It is a hero we welcome back amongst us.'

'Let every Gas Street mouse take note,' said the Chosen mouse in ringing tones, pointing at an embarrassed, but proud Pentecost. 'The oath this friend of mine swore to Zero is null and void. I am told it was taken under duress. Therefore, he will not be granted a full pardon, for he has no crime to answer for. I will now add a few praises of my own. This mouse willingly took my place that I might go out into the countryside to learn the wisdoms of leadership . . . . Or did I take his place? Anyway it doesn't matter, for things turned out right in the end. But the point is, this brave mouse gave up a life of luxury to help us. So let us join our voices in three hearty cheers for one who is amongst the bravest of the brave. And if mine aren't the loudest . . . Hip, hip –.'

'Hooray!' yelled the Gas Street Mob, jumping up to cluster about Pentecost. Young and old, they all took turns to slap him on the back, brushing aside his shyly modest protests. Soon Pentecost himself was cheering with the best of them. So overcome and relieved to be amongst friends was he, he quite forgot that he had news – namely, the death of Zero. He made to mention it, but was interrupted.

'By the way,' said the Chosen mouse, wiping tears of gratitude from his eyes, 'where is our special friend, Fox of Furrowfield, for he is also owed three cheers? You did obey my instructions to wait in the crevice until he came along, uttering the howling signal?'

Pentecost nodded and smiled happily. 'He came just as you said. He should be here quite soon. The last time I saw him he was chasing Black Shadow along the canal. The cockle-snorkle had been telling lies all along. He told me Fox had exchanged my friendship for yours. But now I realise that Fox, being so popular, is bound to have more than one close companion. But I have something more to say. While down in the Basin I saw –.' Again he was interrupted.

'That bug said a lot of things,' said the grim Chosen mouse. 'But he's paying the price, don't worry. He's not shouting his mouth off now.' He turned to nod in the direction of the hole in the wall. Puzzled, Pentecost narrowed his eyes and peered. He saw the shining web. He also saw the large, hairy-legged spider, advancing towards the centre. But whatever could that drab little scrap be, pinned and fluttering upon the bulls-eye? Surely not? But it was.

'Cockle-snorkle!' cried Pentecost. 'What on earth are you doing there? Is this another of your tricks? If so, it's a dangerous one, for you definitely aren't alone. Have you glanced towards your top right yet?'

'Often,' came the bitter reply. 'In fact, I'm having

trouble tearing my eyes away. I think old hairy-shanks has me hypnotized. A trick, you say? You must be joking. But don't fret, I'm resigned to my fate . . . I think.'

'But this is terrible,' said a shocked Pentecost. 'Please, Chosen mouse, we must stop this at once.'

'Why?' said the Chosen mouse, looking surprised. 'He's no friend of yours nor mine. I doubt if he is anyone's friend. Going by his past actions, this insect declared war on the whole world long ago. So why should you wish to save him?'

'It's true I have little to thank him for,' admitted Pentecost. 'But I wouldn't wish to see him end his busy life as a snack.'

'My thoughts exactly!' shouted the bug. 'As soon as you came dashing through that hole I thought, now there's a mouse who cannot bear a grudge. So if you wish to save me, tell the Chosen mouse you love me dearly. But please hurry, for I am beginning to sweat cobs.'

The spider, puzzled, paused to ponder this plea. To occupy himself, he proceeded to patch a frayed portion of his web with odds and ends of silk. But his eyes, or some of them, were fixed anxiously on Pentecost, as that mouse tussled with his emotions. In fact, the spider was known to be a good sport. He was always ready to give folk a fair chance. But he was also a stickler for regular mealtimes. Now he cocked a couple of candid eyes at the Chosen mouse, who was speaking.

'Do you care a fig for that bug after all the misery he has caused?' he asked of Pentecost. 'For that is the condition upon his release. He needs to hear one voice raised in his defence to go free. Are you that voice, Pentecost mouse?'

'I know he has deceived and lied,' said Pentecost hesitantly. 'And I doubt if I can ever truly forgive him, but —.'

That was enough for the spider. Hastily, he began to pack his darning silks away. Soon he stood poised on tip-toe, eager to continue his journey to the centre of the web. He set off in a sidling circle.

'There you go, anticipating!' yelled the bug. 'Be warned, all that glitters is not gold. Don't be in such an all-fired hurry, the mouse hasn't made up his mind yet.'

'I have seen enough of death,' said Pentecost quietly. 'Not minutes ago I saw Zero drown in the canal. Although I cannot bring myself to like and respect that bug, all life is sacred. It is not for us to —.'

'So do something positive!' yelled the bug. 'All this soul-searching is playing havoc with my nerves. Or are you having your bit of fun at my expense? Well, don't expect me to laugh, for I am definitely not in the mood.'

With a sigh, the spider squatted down and glanced wearily at an undecided Pentecost. He had a feeling this was going to take some time. He was right, for the problem of the bug's future was to be shelved for the time being. The Chosen mouse was staring at Pentecost. So too were the now bolt upright Mob. 'You saw Zero drown in the canal?' repeated the Chosen mouse. 'So why didn't you tell us before? Explain.'

And Pentecost did . . . . 'But he slipped from my grasp,' he finished, his eyes downcast.

'And you tried to save him?' cried the incredulous Chosen mouse. 'Do I hear you right? But he tried to kill you. We now know he and the Sneak also murdered your friend the Scout First Class. And yet you tried to save that worthless villain?'

And again Pentecost saw that look he could not forget. He had seen it in the eyes of the doomed Zero. An expression of puzzlement and lack of understanding. For some time the Chosen mouse just stared. Then his gaze shifted to look at the cellar wall. Then slowly the realisation dawned upon him. The Chosen mouse had learned another lesson. To forgive and help an enemy was the real test. And the Gas Street mouse felt humbled in the presence of Pentecost. For that one had braved his trials alone and deserted, and had still been able to feel for others, even in his hour of need. Not so the Gas Street Mob. They were up and dancing and cheering themselves hoarse. Black Shadow was being chased about the town and the hated Zero lay at the bottom of the canal. It took a while before the Chosen mouse could restore order. The huge relief finally expressed itself in a collective sigh as all the tension of the Gas Street Mob melted away.

Even the patient spider seemed moved by it all. He appeared to be smiling as he lounged against his silken threads, like a boxer waiting for the bell. The worried bug saw no such smile. That was a hungry grimace if ever he saw one. 'Very touching,' he said sarcastically. 'So that rat-bag of a mouse has bought it and now it's cockle-snorkle-baiting time again? Well, let's get it over with. And I hope you all come down with sore throats after you've cheered me out of the world.' He gave a brave flicker.

'Perhaps if I said I almost like him, sometimes?' offered Pentecost, his heart going out to the insect who had done his level best to ruin his life. 'I know it isn't the same as love, but it's a step up from stony hate. And he has been thwarted in his wicked interference. He could even have learned a lesson from all this.'

'Oh, I have,' muttered the bug. 'If I get out of this, I

208

shall look where I'm flying in future. But of course I won't get out of it, for that Chosen mouse has had it in for me ever since I sicked Uncle on him in the Lickey Hills. Not a pleasant experience, being savaged by that senile old mouse.'

For a moment the Chosen mouse seemed to waver. Then, as if shrugging off a momentary weakness, he shook his head. As the spider moved in to finish the job, so the bug's saviour arrived in a most unlikely form. For the one who would save his life was the one who hated him most of all.

'Pardon the hooter,' came a hoarse but cheerful voice. A nose pushed inside the cellar, dimming the proceedings somewhat, for the hole in the wall was small and the nose of Fox of Furrowfield rather large. It then gave a twist to make room for the intrusion of a single, bright brown eye. Another jostle and squeeze, and the tip of an ear came poking through the narrow opening. 'Get myself comfy,' wheezed Fox. 'That's it, all systems go. Now then, you lot, is there a mouse in the house who happens not to belong here? Or perhaps one of your sturdy band might have noticed a mouse with untidy ears flashing past your front door? I wouldn't interrupt your celebrations, but he and I are supposed to be making tracks for home.'

'Fox!' shouted Pentecost, jumping up from the pile of soot and rushing across to the entrance. 'I apologise for ever doubting you.'

'I should think so, too,' replied Fox firmly. 'But I'll tell you this, I'm fed up with chasing mice all over the city.'

'And Black Shadow,' pointed out the Chosen mouse, grinning. 'Your friend told us all about it. So how is he doing?'

209

'Licking his wounds and thinking things over,' replied Fox shortly. Then he too grinned. 'Could be that cat will be out of action for some time, so make the most of it. Gather ye cheeses while ye may, and all that. By the way, small doubting Pentecost mouse, did you happen to notice Zero during the scuffle? He didn't cause more trouble, I hope?'

Pentecost looked embarrassed, and muttered something inaudible. The Chosen mouse hurried across to Fox and whispered in his ear.

'I'm not surprised,' said Fox loudly. 'My saintly friend would go through fire to save the Devil himself. He's quite a gutsy mouse when he isn't admiring himself in puddles and feeling sorry for himself. Anyway, I'm delighted everything has turned out right.'

'And so are we. Thanks to you and the Pentecost mouse we city mice can pick up the pieces, and start afresh in peace and happiness,' replied the grateful Chosen mouse. He turned to his Mob who had gone very quiet. Not unnaturally they were awed by the huge red stranger who joked as he blocked up the entrance of their home. 'Don't be afraid,' their leader reassured them. 'Let me introduce my friend and yours, Fox of Furrowfield.'

'Welcome Fox of Furrowfield!' chorused the still nervous mice. 'We thank you from the bottom of our –'

'Yes, well, enough of that,' interrupted Fox hurriedly. 'I'd like to stay longer but we all have things to do that won't wait.'

'And we know what those things are, don't we, Fox?' sang a voice. 'Steel yourself, for you are about to be blackmailed.'

'Now isn't that a pretty sight?' remarked Fox, swivelling his eye upwards. 'Just look who's come unstuck, or do I mean stuck? So who's your hairy friend? Next for the chop, are we? First Zero and Black Shadow, and now you. My, but we are dealing out justice these days. I will miss you on Lickey Top, but then I often lie in my teeth. So blackmail away, though how, I can't imagine.'

'Don't be flip,' retorted the bug. 'My life is at stake here. That is why you are going to help me. As the Pentecost mouse won't, I am relying on you. Now I want you to gaze sincerely at the Chosen mouse and repeat after me, "With my paw on my heart I can truthfully say that this trapped little bug counts where it matters, for beneath his prankishness beats a heart of pure gold." And if by chance you feel you would sooner bite off your tongue, consider a tucked-away glen where budding red poets romp and play . . . . You do want to keep your private life private, Fox?'

'Nice try,' grinned Fox. 'So how do you intend to spread this information? As I see it, your high-flying days are over.'

'I shall tell *him*,' replied the bug, tearing free his spare leg to point dramatically at Pentecost.

'Tell me what?' asked a puzzled Pentecost. Then his anger flared. 'If this blackmail harmed Fox in any way, I would have nothing to do with it.'

'Why should it harm him?' said the bug innocently. 'You *would* like to know where Fox lives? I mean the exact secret spot. Be honest, the subject has vexed you for a long time. How many times have you bitterly wondered why, though Fox can visit you, you are forever barred from his home?'

'It would be like sharing the load,' agreed Pentecost. 'To be able to call on Fox, day or night, would be a luxury indeed.'

'So get into luxury,' urged the bug. 'For I am going

to tell you where Fox can be reached. Imagine the relief to be able to part the leaves of a camouflaging blackberry bush and shout down the den, "Fox, I have a few problems to chew over".'

Fox winced, and then appealed to the Chosen mouse. 'Couldn't you let the bug off with a caution? I'm sure he's sorry for all the trouble he has caused.'

'When our Chosen mouse says something, he means it!' shouted the son of the Scout First Class. 'He will not allow friendship to stand in the way of his decision. If he did that, the rot would begin to set into his new rule. The bug's only hope is for someone to speak in his defence.'

'If our Chosen mouse wavered now, we would begin to think power corrupts,' warned the one-eyed mouse. 'But our faith tells us he will never tread Zero's rocky road to ruin by becoming absolutely bent. We can only sit and nod approvingly as he once again insists that a sponsor for the bug must step forward.'

'I am the mere instrument of my Mob's will,' said the solemn Chosen mouse. 'I have only one ambition in life: that when I step down from the pinnacle of power, I will be forever remembered as Zero the Just. So, Fox of Furrowfield, if those warm words on behalf of the bug stick in your craw, surrender to his blackmail and hang the consequences.'

'Fine words, but we must be realistic,' insisted a desperate Fox. 'Remember, the school I was brought up in placed great emphasis on compromise.'

The bug, gleefully seeing that Fox was weakening, piled it on. Temptingly, he said to Pentecost, 'Just think of those times when Uncle gets under your paws and up your nose? What better than to be able to send him down to Furrowfields with an important message for

Fox? Why, that old mouse could be gone for days. You know how he thrives on long pointless discussions.'

Fox whimpered as he imagined those determined old paws, limping ever nearer his secret paradise.

'I would never abuse Fox's hospitality,' said the mouse, sharply. 'I would only visit him in an emergency. Or perhaps when the weather was fine and I had nothing else to do. Or if I felt he might be in need of bucking up. And there are those occasions when the little ones grow bored of their old picnic spots. A day out at Fox's would be special for them. Of course, I would cherish his privacy, for we are all entitled to that sacred place we call our own, where one can prop up one's paws, and shut out the world.'

The bug was all enthusiasm. 'Let's hear what Fox thinks. Perhaps he can think up some more chummy get-togethers, for I know he keeps his Sundays free. Lucky Fox, to have all those friends,' continued the sly bug. 'And I need only one.'

The spider, glancing at Fox's expression, marched off in disgust to a dark corner. He realised that both justice and his snack were about to go up the spout. As for the mice, they little cared what happened to the bug. They only wished to get rid of these visitors from the countryside, and pick up the threads of their lives. They knew they owed the Pentecost mouse thanks after all he had suffered on their behalf. And they realised how valuable Fox's help had been. But surely that didn't entitle him to shut out the daylight by corking up their home in that disrespectful manner. In truth, grateful or not, they would be glad to see the back of Fox, the Pentecost mouse and the nasty little bug.

At that moment Fox made up his mind. Pentecost's last words had clinched the matter for him. Despite his detestation for the cockle-snorkle, he was not about to see his home and family disrupted for the sake of a lie or two. Gritting his teeth, he looked up at the bug, ignoring the triumph in that one's eyes.

'You have a friend, and may the Lord forgive me,' he said. He glanced across at the Chosen mouse. 'This bug lives only to be the centre of attention,' he said. 'His boasting is just his pathetic need to be noticed. His need to meddle in the affairs of others relieves his own terrible loneliness. His delight in causing distress serves to mask his own, for deep down he is filled with guilt and self-hatred. So, you see, we should not condemn him, but rather offer our pity. Above all others, that rare and lonely cockle-snorkle needs help. He is no devil, but rather a clown. So I say let him go, for you'll surely agree he is the funniest thing you have ever seen.'

One or two small mice began to giggle as the Chosen mouse approached the web, and, assisted by the one-eyed Breaker, began to unravel the sticky strands that bound the bug prisoner. Now sniggers could be heard from the older mice as the bug fluttered unsteadily to perch upon the rafter. There was no sign of triumph or jubilation now, as he began to comb out his cramped wings with his spare leg. For Fox's biting words had gone deep. His old enemy had turned defeat into a victory. Fox had so spoken as to make the bug's talents appear failings. The cockle-snorkle had been dealt the bitterest blow of all. He had been stripped of his posturing and his pride. For a long time he glared savagely down at the up-turned and laughing faces. He saw the Pentecost mouse, his coat streaked with dirt and oil, his paws and floppy ears cut and bleeding. But despite the pain and suffering that still clouded the mouse's eyes, he now wore a broad smile on his face. The Chosen mouse, too. But more humiliating for the sullen bug was to view Fox's lop-sided grin, half in, and half out of the hole in the wall.

Defeated, the bug flew down from the rafter and, squeezing past an amused Fox, emerged into a crisp new dawn. He wished only to escape the mockery, to nurse his bruised ego beneath his slip of bark back home on Lickey Top. He was just about to head off in that direction when a thought occurred to him. Instantly he was his old, intensely curious self. Such was his strange make-up he easily pushed from his mind the humiliation he had just suffered. For he was thinking back, and remembering something he had intended to do. Soon he was making low searching sweeps over the still quiet city. His whoop of triumph indicated he had spied what he sought. . . .

Panting from his exertions the hurrying mouse had reached and passed the city centre some time before dawn. For a moment he had paused to regain his breath. Then, as if obeying some remembered instructions, he spun on the spot a few times before dashing off due west as hard as he could go.

'West then east,' he babbled to himself, unmindful of the traffic whizzing by on either side as his paws sped him along the central white line of the road. 'And now south, a wide circle to the south, and here we are, you subtle little mouse. We've arrived. . . .'

And so the ambitious Sneak had. But then the notorious Spaghetti Junction had always been easy to find. The boast was that its bewildering tangle of ramps and flyovers were the gateway to the world. But for many a hopeful traveller with an eye on distant parts, it had proved otherwise. For the trick lay in getting off it.

Here, then, came the power-lusting Sneak, determined to rebuild his shattered career. His hope was to meet up with a certain old prophet and son, and get himself Chosen. Only then would he be ready to launch himself on an unsuspecting world. For once delivered from this roaring, fume-choked hell, he intended to descend upon the city to prove himself the bloodiest tyrant of all time. Not for a Chosen Sneak a mere Mob to do his bidding. His dream was to recruit a battalion of strong and obedient bully-mice and batter every Mob in the city into submission. That was his terrible ambition. But first he needed to be Chosen.

'Oh poor deluded subtle mouse!' screamed the delighted bug, passing low to skim the crouching Sneak. 'And do you see them, my wistful friend? Do you see the multitudes all bowing down before the newly Chosen one? Shut tight your eyes and dream, but never wake, for all those hopes will turn to ashes if you do. And so farewell, for we will never meet again. . . .'

The Sneak did not look up to watch him go. Huddled against the crash-barrier, he coughed and wiped his smarting eyes. He was not to know that, whether or not

the old prophet and son came plodding along, his
dreams and schemes would founder, here on Spaghetti
Junction. He was unaware that the old hedgehog hated
subtle folk. Soon the sun would climb as high as it ever
would this late time of year. Many dawns would come
and go, and still the Sneak would be here. And then
would arrive that last dawn, heralded by a blood-red
and warning sky. And it would find him all alone, waiting
for his last sun to go down. . . .

16 Returns and Departures

It was time to go home. A fox and a mouse took their
leave of the Gas Street Mob.

'Goodbye, Chosen mouse, or rather Zero the Just,'
called Pentecost, pausing at the entrance and looking
back. 'And may all your cheese raids be successful.'

'If that is the will of destiny,' was the solemn reply.
'And on behalf of the Gas Street Mob I wish you both a
safe journey home. Our best wishes and thanks go with
you. And though we part, the memory of Fox of Furrowfield and the Pentecost mouse will stay forever in our
hearts. Farewell. . . .'

The streets of the early morning city were still empty.
All was quiet save for the trilling of small birds nudging
for space along the telephone wires. A chill mist hung
overhead, glowing golden where the sun pierced
through. Pentecost, longing to catch that first glimpse
of his beloved hills, bowled happily along behind Fox.

He had seen and experienced enough of the squalid city to last a country-loving mouse a lifetime. Suddenly Fox stopped, turned around and spoke to him.

'When I came down to the Basin for you,' he began, his expression curious, 'why, despite the danger, did you choose to come out of hiding? What was on your mind when you attempted to save Zero? You know quite well he would have done for you, had the chance arisen. So why did you do it?'

Pentecost replied haltingly. Thinking back he was not sure himself. 'I hated Zero, and yet . . . when I saw him cuffed about by Black Shadow, and when he toppled over the bank, all my hatred went. I just couldn't watch him drown, Fox. But I still detest his memory. He did many terrible and wicked things. But for those few moments when he was struggling for his life . . . oh, I just don't know why I did it, Fox. . . .'

'But you did,' said Fox wonderingly. Then he was all grins. 'But come on, don't let's brood about it any more. What's past is past. And you have learnt your lesson, I hope. For it wasn't so glamorous was it? The adventurous trip to the city, I mean? We all did a lot of dashing about, and Heaven knows how many thousands of noble words were spouted, and still there is not one hero in sight. Can you see one?'

'I have no wish to make your ears burn, Fox,' said Pentecost, slyly. 'I know how you hate warm compliments.'

Fox tried to look stern. 'Listen, nuisance, in this life we can only do our best. We get into scrapes, and wriggle out as well as we can. If we happen to help others whilst looking after our own skins, it's by the way. . . .'

'If we can help somebody as we pass along, then our

living will not be in vain,' said Pentecost, understanding, and hurrying after the trotting Fox. 'Honestly, your wisdom never ceases to amaze me.'

'And you can leave out the jokes,' called Fox over his shoulder. 'It's homeward-bound time so step lively. I don't know about you but I'm starving.' And he increased his pace out of the city, the cheerful mouse puffing along behind.

Soon, thankfully, they were sneaking along the last street, were plunging into the wilderness of grass and shrubs that bordered that final barrier to the open countryside: the great black road. Once there, at Fox's prompting, they sat side by side on its kerb. Every time Pentecost asked why they had stopped he was told to shut up. And so he did, impatiently staring up at Fox, who was staring up the road as if waiting for something. Quite soon along it came, a huge and swaying vehicle, its lights blazing as it lumbered slowly through the mists. As it neared, Pentecost could make out its load of tiered cages, strewing behind what appeared to be small flurries of snow. Just before it passed, Fox seized the mouse and flung him unceremoniously aboard, then leapt up to join him. Instantly panic broke out amongst the caged passengers. Feathers flew and voices were raised together in cackled protest. At this point, fearing the worst, the mouse turned his head away and stared at the road. As the city receded and the foothills of the Lickies hove into view, so Fox licked his chops, his hungry eyes wandering from cage to cage. This was the way to travel, he mused. In style, and with a good breakfast inside one. . . .

Shortly after dawn an old mouse and a newly-returned bug held a whispered conversation. Moments later the

old mouse set feverishly to work. His vigour must have been extremely taxing for a mouse of his advanced age, but he had fear for a spur. The bug, his smile devilishly wide, was perched upon one of the few still-upright grass-stems, a mere pin-point of light in the gloom. There was a malicious gleam in the insect's eye as he watched Uncle tearing up pawfuls of grass, twigs, and other building materials. He had returned in a vengeful mood to frighten the oldster out of his wits, and thus to cause more trouble. For after listening to the bug, Uncle had become a desperate mouse indeed. As the sun rose and the mists cleared he began to attract an audience, for it was unusual to see Uncle working hard, if at all. Soon the small mice were sitting in a semi-circle, their eyes wide as they viewed their Uncle's handiwork.

'Some of you might be wondering why I'm building this?' he panted, looking haggard and worn.

'All of us are,' said one youngster. 'At a guess I would say it is either for law and order purposes, or a sports facility for us to jump over.'

'No mouse will jump this when it's finished,' promised a grim Uncle. 'Not even a city-hardened one, with a bitter grudge against me. When that merciless Pentecost returns he will get a shock. This is a siege barrier for him to crash into when he makes a bee-line for me. This kind bug has warned me in advance about that evil Pentecost's plans. He believes I have taken over his job, and has sworn vengence.'

'But you have taken over his job,' came the innocent response. 'Don't you wish to be called Uncle Pentecost any more?'

'I can't understand it!' cried a bewildered Uncle. 'I was only holding the reins of leadership taut until he came home. So why is he hurrying back in a state of great excitement to confront me snout to snarling snout? Why does he vow that there will be bits of flying mouse everywhere before he is finished with me? Oh, what a personal problem,' he moaned, shaking his old head.

'Perhaps if we tested your crash barrier for you?' offered the little ones. They scrambled to their paws. 'We will attempt to charge through it.' Instantly they had hurled themselves against the fragile looking barrier, effortlessly bursting through in several places. Uncle, a dejected figure, had made no move to stop them. There was a dull and resigned expression in his eyes as he watched his hastily built protection quickly reduced to a hastily destroyed nothingness.

'Which is as it should be,' remarked Old Mother. 'The only good barrier is a flat one. One day there will be no such things as barriers. And what a better place the world will be for it. How comforting that the young should recognise this truth.'

'And enjoy making it a fact!' shouted the small wreckers.

'So it will be a bristling face to face?' sighed Uncle. 'And I will end up as bits of flying mouse, no doubt? Oh, what a welcome home I would have given the Pentecost mouse, had he allowed it. I would have hobbled to meet him with pawfuls of ripe blackberries in the spirit of generosity. But what is the use with all these black marks piling up against me?'

'I will never forget the blackest one of all,' sniffed an aunt. 'I remember the time when the family journeyed here to escape the over-spilling city. It was Uncle who ruined the shape of Pentecost's ears when he attempted to cure them, just outside Woodpecker Wood. I doubt if he has ever forgiven you for that.'

222

'I only twiddled them a little,' protested Uncle. 'How was I to know it would lead to him hating what he saw in puddles for the rest of his life?'

'I can see grudge piling on grudge,' warned the aunt. 'But then Pentecost himself has a lot to answer for when he arrives home. Destiny or not, he did desert us, and without a word spoken. And what did we get back in his place?'

'A good-for-nothing Chosen mouse, who was never what he seemed,' said Old Mother, gazing at a black cloud in the sky. 'I have never known such troubled times as these.' Uncle grimaced. He was toying with the idea of going into hiding.

Just then the Old Codger and Son hove into sight. Uncle cheered up at once. He was in need of a friend at this moment. Perhaps the hedgehogs could get him out of this mess. But if they couldn't there was always the escape plan simmering in his mind. He was thinking of a long and winding tunnel, with a false entrance or two. . . . 'Old Codger and Son,' he greeted them warmly. 'And how is the precious gift this morning? Has it tuned into any messages that might please an elderly mouse's heart? Any encouraging snippet concerning the state of his future health would do.'

'Talking about health,' said the Son, halting at the edge of the circle and proceeding to scratch, 'I am pleased to announce that my dad feels in the pink this morning. He has fallen over only once since sunrise, and that was an accident. He stumbled into a crater he didn't know was there.'

'Accident?' scoffed the bug. 'He falls into a hole he dug himself and calls it an accident? I must warn you Owl is at the end of his tether, and mad with rage at the moonscape you've made of his velvet grassy slopes.'

'Very well, if we must split hairs,' said the Son coolly. 'Perhaps his accident was self-inflicted. However, I was overjoyed to note that he sprang back on his feet in a twinkling. If that isn't feeling in the pink, I don't know what is. In fact he feels so fit this morning he has arrived at a decision. And speaking of Owl, my dad has a bit of good news for him, too. But first things first. Because he feels so fit, my dad has decided not to –.'

'Please excuse me for butting in,' said an anxious Uncle. 'But I have a serious personal problem. I need to know whether the Pentecost mouse is returning in a forgiving mood. The bug says that mouse has it in for me, but I would value a second opinion from the gift.'

Obligingly, the Son took up his listening post. For once the Old Codger's jaws weren't chewing. Not so strange, really, for anyone with eyes could see that the nettle-beds of Lickey Top had been picked as clean as a whistle. If there was a single snail left on Owl's property, it was extremely good at hiding.

'What's that, Dad?' said the Son, holding his breath so as to catch the barely audible whisper. 'A mouse is returning from the city. . . . He will not be what he seems. . . . And he will be the cause of great . . . sorry, the gift's packed up again.'

'Destiny is repeating itself,' wailed Old Mother. 'Heaven forbid that we are to be fobbed off with another Chosen mouse. Is there nothing straightforward and seemly in this world?'

'The power's come back,' shushed the Son. 'How's that, Dad . . . the returning mouse will not be in a forgiving mood, for –?'

That was enough for Uncle. His nerves finally snapped. 'I'm done for!' he shouted, limping about in agitation. 'The Old Codger's message is as clear as crystal.

The Pentecost mouse will approach me with an unseemly smile on his face, but inside he will be quaking with temper. His plan will be to sidle to my worst, bad paw side, and then pounce to be the cause of great suffering. To think, just when a mouse of my age should be snoozing quietly, life suddenly becomes a race against time. Ah, that this should happen to your old Uncle who has always believed in non-violence. Well, there is only one thing to be done –.'

'If you will let my dad finish,' said the impatient Son. 'There is some more of the message.'

'I have heard enough,' said Uncle sadly. 'It is time for me to find a quiet spot over Wending Way. There I will scrape out a small hole just big enough to hold one old mouse, plus paws. When the Pentecost mouse arrives just tell him he drove me to it, for you will never see me again.'

'You can tell him yourself!' cried a youngster, pointing down the hill. 'For if that isn't Fox emerging from the wood and if that isn't by his side our leader – who has changed colour for some reason – then I'll go to the foot of Owl's tree.' At these words, Uncle let out a yell and set off for the brow of Lickey Top hill as fast as his bound-up paws could carry him.

The small mouse was correct. Toiling up the slope came Fox. Beside him marched a mouse of a most unusual hue.

'Heaven preserve us,' whispered Old Mother. 'The fear in the city has turned our Pentecost a whiter shade of pale. I knew that black cloud boded ill. For a more unseemly soul I have never seen. I doubt if he will be the cause of great rejoicing in that condition, though that was my hope. What a tragedy that the Old Codger should hit the unseemly nail on the head, and miss the other.'

'I've never known folk to jump to conclusions like Harvest mice,' said the bewildered Son, shaking his head. 'If only Uncle had let my dad finish. For the whole message was, "The mouse will not be in a forgiving mood, for there is nothing to forgive." So why should he up and run that way?'

'Because that is Uncle,' replied an Aunt simply. 'He does extraordinary things to stay in the limelight. He will be holed up somewhere, waiting to be forgiven and led home. But look, whatever gave our Pentecost the idea that that city fashion would suit him?'

The family fell silent as the travellers neared. Wordlessly, they parted to allow the pair to enter the circle. Fox looked tired, but quite happy. Then all eyes centred upon the returned leader. Only then was his appearance explained. He had, for some reason, chosen to roll first in mud and oil, and then in white chicken feathers. Most of the mice fell in with the aunt's opinion. If that was how city folk sported themselves, then a mouse was better off in the old traditional countryside, where plainness spoke louder than gaudiness. They also noted that Fox had adopted the style, but in a toned-down way. He had settled for a neat little fringe of white feathers around his jaws. Then Pentecost was smiling, though hesitantly. He opened his mouth to speak, but Old Mother beat him to it. She asked her burning question.

'Whatever have you been playing at?' she said gently. But her eyes were filled with hope as the wind changed, as that black cloud came drifting back, its edges now lined with shining silver.

Pentecost was looking slowly around him, at the churned-up slopes of Lickey Top, at the neglected homes, so neat and tidy when he had left. Then he drew

226

himself up, a quiet fire burning in his eyes. Despite his unkempt and half-starved appearance, there was about him the air of a mouse who had learned much these past few days.

'I left for the city a discontented and vain mouse,' he began. 'I return humbled, and begging your forgiveness. What have I been playing at? At the game of life, Old Mother, and I have learned many lessons. Never again will I yearn to be a hero in your eyes, for I am a simple mouse, and not cut out for such things. As I look about me I can see what my true role in life is. For as destiny prepared the Chosen mouse for his great mission in the city, so I was also taken from my home to be moulded into a leader worthy of you. I will only say that I am thankful to be home, and hope that you will find it in your hearts to think kindly of me.'

Kindness, forgiveness, thankfulness: all these feelings the harvest mice of Lickey Top gave vent to in a burst of happy cheering. They surrounded their leader, protesting that they had always believed in him, and that in the future they would try not to ignore him so much.

'Great stuff, eh?' said the bug, eyeing Fox warily. He continued in a pally voice, 'And it's all thanks to you. Heroes come and heroes go, but Fox goes on forever, eh? And so dignified you are with it. Proudly standing aside with your jaws shut tight while the Pentecost mouse gets the credit for a mission impossible. But what a tale we could tell, eh, Fox?'

'And you did,' Fox growled. Then sarcastically, 'I notice you weren't so chirpy in the Gas Street cellar this morning. And a word in the ear, never attempt to blackmail me again.'

'No sense of humour, that's your trouble,' said the suddenly sulky bug. For a while he swayed on his grass

227

stem, sullenly brooding. He was bored again, but not for long. He was remembering the Son speaking of a decision his father had arrived at, and also something about Owl. Eyes bright and curious now, he glanced across at the young hedgehog who was watching the happy reunion of the harvest mice through thickly-fringed eyes. 'What were you saying about your dad, and Owl?' questioned the bug. 'Don't keep it to yourself, spoil-sport.'

'I've been trying to tell all of you,' the Son retorted. 'But no-one would listen.'

'Order!' shouted the cockle-snorkle. 'The Son has more vital news for us.' The hub-bub from the celebrating harvest mice died down. Soon they were listening intently, for news of any kind always caused them to cock up their ears.

'My dad has decided not to die this year,' said the Son loudly. 'He thinks that next year might be a better time. You see, his health crisis was a false alarm. He is now in the pink which is why he has set his heart on another trip around the world. But this time he fancies to view it from a fresh angle. Still with a compassionate eye, of course, for despite the state of the world he still feels hope for it. His only fear is that the subtle folk might one day get the upper hand. For it is that type who have made the world the cynical place it is. That's why he detests cockle-snorkles, and takes kindly to the Uncle types.'

'Thanks for nothing,' sneered the bug. 'But don't think you can fool me. All this dying in the land of one's birth rubbish. You came up here to clean Owl out of snails. And as like as not you'll be here next year to do it again. So who is going to fill in all those burial holes you won't be needing? But never mind – give with

Owl's good news, for Heaven knows he's badly in need of some.'

'Don't you imply that my dad is a con artist,' bristled the Son. 'His illness was genuine. Not so Owl's, alas. For my dad has told me to apologise for the unnecessary pain the bird has suffered. In fact his nail hasn't grown inwards at all. That too was a false alarm. What Owl regards with horror is the natural state of things. For the nails of owls are meant to turn up, as the owner should well know. I'm afraid the gift made a mistake. The pain Owl endures exists only in his mind. If it's any consolation, he could plan a hunting trip for this very night and pull it off without any ill effects.'

There came a loud in-drawing of breath as all eyes turned up to view the black hole in the oak, and the limp foot dangling outside it. Owl had heard every word, for the foot gave a tentative twitch, then another. Then it began to flex smoothly, and with growing confidence. The watching mice agreed that a healthier foot they had yet to see. But their comments masked a certain nervousness, for they were awaiting the reaction that was bound to follow. And then it came. There sounded a bellow of rage and anguish from that dark interior. Not a cry of gladness, for Owl seemed unamused by his change of fortune.

The bug, pretending concern, flew to perch on the edge of his master's home. He peered inside. 'They've pulled a fast one, Owl,' he sympathised. 'It was all a cunning trick to keep you on your back while they rifled all your pretty sections. And rifled it they have, look you. Now Lickey Top is just a swamp with craters where once bloomed wild flowers. And what did the Pentecost mouse do against your orders? Instead of holding the fort, he chose to race off to the city. That's where I was, Owl, trying to persuade him to return and do his duty. But did he? You can't trust anyone these days, Owl. Except me, of course. So are the pains in your mind easing off? That would at least be something. And you can also look forward to a good supper tonight. You must be famished, Owl.'

'Famished?' yelled the bird, his pouched and sleepless eyes glaring wildly down at the circle beneath his tree. 'Of course I'm famished. But do you seriously believe I could force a thing down, after being to hell and back? Food would gag in my throat. No, I want those flea-ridden vandals off my land at once, or I won't be responsible for my actions. And as for that ridiculously feathered mouse, I'd advise him to buckle down and get my property cleaned up. And quick, too, unless he and his whinging tribe fancy a trip around the world with those two.'

'We will have it looking as pretty as a picture,' comforted Pentecost. 'Don't apologise for your harsh words, Owl, we appreciate what you've been through. But you can now rest assured that everything is back to normal. I intend to stay home and buckle down to my duties from now on. You know I was sent into the city by destiny, and almost came a cropper? It all started when –.'

'Save it,' snapped the bird. He cocked a mean eye at the Old Codger and Son. 'And why are they still here?'

'I am in the process of turning my dad around,' said the indignant Son. 'Once I get his nose pointed in the direction of the Weasel Woods, he will be off like the wind. He just needs a coaxing start, that's all. It's just that his reflexes are a bit slow, having gone without lunch this morning.'

Soon the Old Codger was levelled up, his blank eyes

focused on the tree-line below. 'It's goodbye, then?' said the Son. 'My dad says it will be good to feel the firmness of Spaghetti Junction beneath his paws. His only hope is that we don't run into any subtle folk as we journey round and round and round the world.'

'I don't believe you've ever gone round the world,' sneered the bug. 'You just plod round the Junction until the snail season is at its height.'

Calmly, the Son studied the insect for a long moment, his thickly fringed eyes never once blinking. Then without a word he turned and set off down the hill, his father ambling along in his wake.

Owl watched them go, his beak clicking with satisfaction. Not until they had actually ambled into the wood did his suspicious eyes return to the mice at the foot of his tree. 'Right,' he said, indicating the churned-up slopes of Lickey Top. 'You lot can get your heads down, and clean up all this mess. And quietly, if you don't mind, for I have some thinking to do.'

'You really shouldn't speak to us like that, Owl,' protested Pentecost. 'Our lives are just as important as yours. We too have gone through a traumatic experience.'

'And what is even more sad, Uncle Pentecost is still going through his,' said a small mouse. 'Because of that bug's lying, he has now become a hunted fugitive. It is now the task of our leader to track him down and flush him out with a sharp stick, for taking his name in vain.'

'I thought my home-coming was too tranquil,' said Pentecost, only just realising that Uncle had gone missing. Then he looked stern. 'But you talk nonsense. I don't hold a grudge against Uncle. Which way did he go?'

The youngster pointed out the still-fresh trail. At

once, Pentecost hurried off towards Wending Way. Fox, determined not to miss this for the world, trotted after him, grinning. Ignoring Owl's angry comments, and the sharp scoldings from the bug, the harvest mice contentedly set to clearing up Lickey Top. They tackled one crater at a time, digging up pawfuls of earth with which to fill them in. In this way they succeeded in filling in one hole, only to create another. But if their work was slapdash, it was at least a labour of love. For Lickey Top was not only Owl's home, but their home, too. As they cheerfully bustled, so the events of the past troubled-filled days receded from their minds. Safe in the knowledge that Pentecost was home and in charge once more, they were already thinking about tomorrow. For there was so much to do with the days so short, and winter coming on. Amid laughter and song, a memorable day lengthened; but slowly, as if reluctant to give away to the quietly slumbering night. . . .

Dejectedly, Uncle watched the stream race by. He had chosen to hide out beneath the exposed roots of a weeping willow tree, some way down the bank. It was not a wise choice. No sooner had the old mouse crammed himself inside than he began to sink. Already the sticky mud was slopping around his paws, and rising higher every moment. Whatever had he done to deserve such a fate, he moaned? Was he to die all alone for making two small mistakes? He had only jokingly called himself Uncle Pentecost, he reasoned piteously. But the second mistake was plain silliness. To hide out in a sinking bog, of all places. The way things were going the mud would be up to his nose before long, and then what? Too late now to return and throw himself upon the mercy of Pentecost, for the sucking mud would not let him go.

At this moment he would have welcomed the appearance of a sharply poking stick, for Uncle was ever a grasper of straws. He listened hopefully, and shook his head. He had been straining to hear the patter of rescuing paws. But it seemed there would be no help for a favourite Uncle this time. Soon he would utter a final gurgle before vanishing for ever beneath the ooze. What a destiny, he groaned. There would be no-one to know that he had died blowing bubbles, as if life was a game. Weakly, he attempted to pull a paw from the gobbling mud, only to be drawn further into the slime. Now he knew what death was like, he thought despairingly. Listlessly, he tried to pull his other paw free, and down he sank again. But then Uncle was not the kind of mouse who learned from his mistakes.

It was then he heard voices. 'Uncle, Uncle where are you?' they called. And then just one of the voices, the deeper one. 'Where are you, you silly old fool?' Could he be in heaven already, he wondered, or just nearly? For those voices sounded very ghostly to his imaginative mind. With a sigh, the old mouse waited for the end. Now he could hear the sharp sound of snapping twigs. With an effort he twisted his head to peer up the bank. It was then his terrified eyes took in the ghostly white mouse peering down at him. Was he to be haunted, too, even before he was dead, he thought miserably? The voices again, but with a sense of relief Uncle recognised the unmistakable tones of Pentecost. Now the white leader was joined by the looming red shape of a grinning Fox. Uncle set his snout stubbornly. If they were expecting to find a mouse with his pride stripped away, they would be disappointed.

Pentecost spoke. 'I wish Uncle would grasp the end of this twig,' he said, anxiously. 'For we would dearly love to haul him to safety. He cannot realise how badly he is needed to supervise all the clearing up on Lickey Top.'

'If he would grab this life-saving twig we could draw him from the mud like a rotten old tooth,' came Fox's amused voice. 'On the other hand, if he prefers to sink, we could throw him both ends and go home. Some old mice like pottering about in mud, so they say.'

'Uncle, the twig is coming down!' shouted Pentecost. 'Take no notice of Fox, he is joking, as usual. Come on now, no-one is angry with you.'

Uncle watched as the twig came poking down amongst the roots of the willow tree. Reaching out he gripped it tightly. Slowly he was yanked from the ooze. No sooner had he regained a firm footing than he gave the twig a crafty tug. Pentecost, still holding on to the other end, gave a yell, over-balanced and fell with a splash into the stream. The swift current surged around him, taking with it a slick of oily feathers.

'So much for the ghostly Pentecost,' remarked a satisfied Uncle. 'Perhaps in future you will learn to stop dead instead of dashing off to the city. And as for the supervising job, I have never been a menial labouring mouse, and I don't intend to become one. It is your fault Lickey Top is in such a mess, so you and Furrowfield can clear it up. I have more important things to do.' And so saying he limped off up Wending Way hill, trailing mud and fuming. Upon reaching home he got down to the important business of a good snooze.

'That's another lesson we've learned,' said Fox, hauling his now-clean friend to safety. 'Never expect thanks from ungrateful old mice.' He turned and began to lope off. 'Race you to the top!' he challenged. Happiness lent them wings. In a few bounds Fox reached the top of the hill; Pentecost, wet but contented, coming in a valiant second.

17 In Country Heaven

The sun was setting over the Lickey Hills. A shadow flapped across its glowing face as Owl set off for his hunting grounds along the Great River. The breeze, dashing the few remaining leaves from the oaks, the slim poplar, the ash, moaned as if warning of approaching winter. Only the straight pines would stay unchanged and evergreen through the coming frosts and ice and snow. Pentecost shivered to feel the nip in the air. Silently he and Fox watched the rise of a silver cold moon. Wide and clear, the sky was flecked with stars, glittering like chips of ice. Instinctively, the friends knew there would be few more perfect nights like this. Soon the winds would blow from the north, and the clouds would bank up, sullen and grey from horizon to horizon. Pentecost gazed out from their high place at a smudge of light, glowing like a beacon in a dark, faraway country. Raising a paw, he seemed fascinated that he could so easily blot from view that brilliance which fed upon the miseries of the less fortunate. But as long as he lived, Pentecost would never be able to blot the city from his mind. Turning to Fox he made to speak, but his friend had his eyes tight shut, as if in sleep.

But in fact Fox was quite awake. He was concentrating upon a thought-poem that was forming in his mind. With a bit of polishing it would slot nicely into 'The Ballad of Fox of Furrowfield', he mused. He thought it once more . . . .

> Loping, belly gnawing hollow,
> Slinking, slyly slipping follow,
> Stealthy stealing, chops a-licking,
> Winking at a little chicken . . . .

The last line was intended to appease the anti-fox brigade, though Fox doubted that it would. In some, the hatred for foxes was too deeply ingrained, and for them 'The Ballad' would never hold meaning. But then such was life. Fox opened his eyes to find himself alone. . . .

Motionless, Pentecost sat beside the small mount that contained the earthly remains of that old heroic leader. Would that odd-eyed mouse have approved of him, he wondered? Would he have thought him a worthy successor? For in his own eyes he had proved himself a failure in the city. Surely the truly courageous would have overcome the fear that had haunted him throughout that time? It was then the voice spoke to him. And Pentecost listened to the inner mouse he had so long ignored.

'Pentecost,' it said. 'Fate sent an envious and selfish mouse into the city and brought him back much humbled and wiser. Be proud that you are not an imitation of Pentecost gone, but a leader in your own right. For though you trod the city streets in fear, you sought to help both friend and foe. Yours was not the hero's triumph over others, but something rarer. You fought that fear to help a friend, and stifled loathing to show pity for an enemy. Your struggle was the noblest of them all: against yourself. Stand tall, for like the Chosen mouse you have a task before you. For your mission is not ended, but merely begun. Even now the family sing your praises. This is their need, for you are their hope and strength. But listen . . . .'

And Pentecost listened. What had been a muted hum from the grass-spun homes of the harvest mice, was now suddenly loud and clear in his ears:

'We chose him with his raggedy ears from many, and we chose not wrong. . . .'

'For within are the qualities of a Pentecost gone, though not forgotten,' was the firm agreement.

'He is a hero,' said a small, waking mouse.

'Perhaps,' answered that first voice. 'But of the quieter kind. Now go to sleep. . . .'

The wind howled, and the voices of the family were no longer heard. And Pentecost, both moved and glad, vowed to that inner mouse many things. And the inner mouse was contented. At that moment, was it imagination that Pentecost saw a shadow, slipping across the hill, the moonlight glinting in a pair of oddly-coloured eyes? Was it just a trick of the light? Yet another had seen it, too.

'So here you are,' said Fox, sliding from behind. 'And who was that, and why did he go so suddenly? Surely not afraid of a large red shape?'

'Can a hero fear a hero?' asked Pentecost, smiling mysteriously. 'Or even the shadow of one?'

'So let you and I chase shadows,' said Fox, with a grin. 'It's a lovely night for it.'

Together they set off down the hill. 'I was thinking about that poem you and I meant to compose,' said Pentecost suddenly. 'I suggest it should be about the coming of snow, the going of snow, and a mouse tingling in the first warmth of spring. It will be called "The Mouse in Winter".'

'How about "The Fox and the Mouse in Winter"?' said Fox, the expert poet. 'There is more snap in that title, don't you think?'

'It does hint at a certain warmth,' admitted Pentecost. 'The Mouse and the Fox in Winter" it shall be.'

Fox nodded cheerfully. 'Good. So while you and I and the weather turn around, let us scour the country-side beneath our personal moon. Epic poems need to be thoroughly researched, you see.'

And Fox and Pentecost set off through the Lickey Hills in search of inspiration. They were not alone. It was not fancy that they saw in every dell, on each new rise, flitting from tree to tree as if to mock mere death, the ever-present shadow of a hero. And the two, the three friends wended the hills, companions for always, in joy and sorrow . . . through country Heaven . . . .

W J Corbett

THE SONG OF PENTECOST

Winner of the Whitbread Award

Set in the hills, valleys, woodlands and rubbish dumps of the Midlands, *The Song of Pentecost* is a story of a journey against great odds.

A tribe of harvest mice, led by Pentecost and with the help of Snake and Frog, leave their wasteland home for the Oily Green Pool and Lickey Top where they hope to have a brighter, greener future.

But the journey to Oily Green Pool is fraught with danger; amongst the obstacles the mice encounter is a river, Ambush Path which is the home of an aggressive tribe of renegade mice known as the Ruffians, Woodpecker Woods and Snake's unsavoury cousin.

'An astonishing achievement. I read it with delight...'

Roald Dahl

'A story full of wit, quirky humour and poetry...'
Observer

W J Corbett

PENTECOST OF LICKEY TOP

The Orphan of the Lake means trouble for Lickey Top, for orphan Otter is a bully and thief.

When the orphan is encouraged to follow his lucky star and set up home in the Lickey Hills, Owl threatens the harvest mice with eviction.

Is this the chance their leader Pentecost has been waiting for? Can he prove he is the hero he dreams of being? With his old friend Fox of Furrowfield, can he save the hilltop paradise or will they both fall victim to the ambitions of the younger generation?

This is the stunning conclusion to the award-winning *Song of Pentecost* trilogy.

"Mr W J Corbett is a born writer."
Auberon Waugh, *Daily Mail*

W J Corbett

THE END OF THE TALE AND OTHER STORIES

The sixteen stories in this collection all have animal characters, including a hare who doesn't like to be hugged, a spider who spends a lifetime spinning socks for a centipede and a young, mischievous giraffe.

A feast of entertainment for all readers, young and old alike, by the author of *Dear Grumble, Duck Soup Farm, Little Elephant, Toby's Iceberg* and *The Song of Pentecost,* winner of the Whitbread Award.

Vivien Alcock

TRAVELLERS BY NIGHT

Peachem's Circus is closing down and the circus folk are faced with changing their glitter and spangles for the ordinary world. Charlie and Belle are to be sent to live with an aunt and go to school - until they find out that Tessie, the old circus elephant, is facing a rather grimmer fate.

In desperation, the two children kidnap the elephant and set off on a journey that is both frightening and exciting.

By the author of *The Trial of Anna Cotman*, shortlisted for the Carnegie Medal, *A Kind of Thief, The Stonewalkers* and *The Sylvia Game*.

Colin Dann

THE ANIMALS OF FARTHING WOOD

"We must face the facts!" Toad cried... "Farthing Wood is finished; in another couple of years it won't even exist. We must all find a *new* home. Now - before it's too late!"

When men arrive with bulldozers in Farthing Wood, its animals and birds know that their world is doomed. The only chance for Badger, Toad, Kestrel and the others is a perilous cross-country trek towards a new life in a nature reserve. But not even Fox, their brave and intelligent leader, is prepared for all the dangers that lie ahead. And when disaster strikes the group, their new home seems an impossible dream...

Winner of the Arts Council National Book Award

Jack London

WHITE FANG

Born in the frozen wilds of north-west Canada, White Fang, 3/4 wolf, is the only survivor of the cold and hunger which kill his litter-mates.

Falling into the hands of mankind as a youngster, he becomes first a sled dog, then a fighter before his unexpected rescue from the harsh and savage world he was born into.

Jack London's tale of White Fang's fight for survival is one of the greatest animal stories ever written.

John Masefield

THE MIDNIGHT FOLK

When Kay Harker sets out to discover the long-lost family treasure, his friends The Midnight Folk gather to help him. The Midnight Folk are Kay's toys - Nibbins the black cat, Bitem the fox, Blinky the owl and a whole tribe of other friends which had been locked away with the arrival of his new governess.

Kay's nightly investigations into the treasure lead him and The Midnight Folk into a world of mystery and adventure.

The Box of Delights, and its prequel, *The Midnight Folk,* were described by the *Times* as "two of the greatest children's books ever written."

John Masefield

THE BOX OF DELIGHTS

On his way home from school for the Christmas holidays, Kay Harker meets a mysterious Punch and Judy man on the train. The man gives Kay the magic Box of Delights. The Box takes Kay into the past, into the days of King Arthur and beyond that, to the ancient city of Troy.

But wicked Abner Brown is also after the Box and pursues Kay through time to try and steal the Box away from him. Kay must protect the Box of Delights at all costs - but is he any match for Abner Brown?

Michael Morpurgo

LITTLE FOXES

Billy Bunch, uncared for and unloved, discovers a secret wilderness by a ruined church. The wilderness and the animals he finds there give a new focus to his life. When his secret place is discovered and the last fox threatened by hunters, Billy doesn't hesitate to join in its flight.

By the author of *Why the Whales Came*, now a major film.

Michael Morpurgo

THE NINE LIVES OF MONTEZUMA

"Monty? Why Monty?" his mother asked.
"Montezuma, the Aztec King. He was a survivor, a
great fighter. I read about him last term in history."

From the moment of his birth in the farmyard,
Montezuma is a survivor. From his unfortunate
encounter with a tin can to his fight with the
farm's dog and on through his various adventures
as he roams the farmyard and the fields beyond,
he gradually changes, through his nine lives of
danger and excitement, from fiery kitten to a tired
old tom-cat always independent, a law unto
himself.

A Selected List of Fiction from Mammoth

While every effort is made to keep prices low, it is sometimes necessary to increase prices at short notice. Mandarin Paperbacks reserves the right to show new retail prices on covers which may differ from those previously advertised in the text or elsewhere.

The prices shown below were correct at the time of going to press.

All these books are available at your bookshop or newsagent, or can be ordered direct from the address below. Just tick the titles you want and fill in the form below.

Cash Sales Department, PO Box 5, Rushden, Northants NN10 6YX.
Fax: 0933 410321 : Phone 0933 410511.

Please send cheque, payable to 'Reed Book Services Ltd.', or postal order for purchase price quoted and allow the following for postage and packing:

£1.00 for the first book, 50p for the second; **FREE POSTAGE AND PACKING FOR THREE BOOKS OR MORE PER ORDER.**

NAME (Block letters) ....

ADDRESS ....

....

☐ I enclose my remittance for ....

☐ I wish to pay by Access/Visa Card Number

Expiry Date

Signature ....

Please quote our reference: MAND